Everyone Needs An Algonquin

Everyone Needs An Algonquin

*The Collected Wit And Wisdom Of
Agatha Whitt-Wellington (Miss)*

Foreword by Rupert Stanley Quim

Through The Split Window
©2013

Everyone Needs An Algonquin
Agatha Whitt-Wellington (Miss)

Copyright © 2013 Through The Split Window

ISBN-13: 978-0615820460 (Through The Split Window)
ISBN-10:0615820468

Printed in the United States of America

First Edition: May 2013

Email OnAgathasBehalf@gmail.com or
visit EveryoneNeedsAnAlgonquin.com.

DEDICATION

*It's impossible to thank everyone who has inspired me so I shan't even
bother trying, but I feel obliged to send a kiss to all of my Christophers
-- particularly Robert, Mitch and the other one.*

TABLE OF CONTENTS

FOREWORD: *Agatha, The Miss Behind The Myth*

A
ACCEPTANCE: *Minds Are Like Parachutes --*   2
     Made Out Of Relatively Flimsy Material
ADVICE: *Do As I Say*   4
ART: *Throwing Down Gang Signs For Dummies*   7

B
BEAUTY: *The Gorgeousness Within*   10
BELONGING: *My Cobbled Road To Damascus*   12
BETRAYAL: *Separating The Lights From The Dark*   15

C
CLARITY: *Memo To All Idiots -- Stop Being Idiots*   20
COMPANIONSHIP: *My Relationship With*   22
     The Lesser Species
COURTSHIP: *Dreams And Worship In The Summer Sun*   25

D
DIPLOMACY: *Cruel To Be Kind*   30
DISTINCTION: *There's You And Then There's Me*   33
DUALITY: *Perpetually An Expatriate*   35

E
ELOQUENCE: *Wise Words From A Dead Man*   38
ENCOURAGEMENT: *Inspiration And Sage Advice*   39
     For Budding Scribes
ETIQUETTE: *A Packet Of Crisps And A Pint Of Winkles*   41

F
FITNESS: *I Worry About You, You Know*   46
FOCUS: *Baby, You Can Drive My Car*   47
FRIENDSHIP: *Everyone Needs An Algonquin*   49

G

GLORY: *The Weird And Wonderful -- The City Centre*   52
GRACE: *Where Was His Stethoscope?*   54
GRATITUDE: *Thank You, Driver, For Getting Me Here*   57

H

HANKY PANKY: *You Love It And You Know It*   60
HEALTH: *It Does A Body Good*   62
HOME: *A Welcome Mat*   64

I

INCOME: *Money, It's A Gas*   68
INTERACTION: *Woo And How To Pitch It*   70
INTIMIDATION: *Are You Being Bullied?*   73

J

JEOPARDY: *Health And Safety Be Damned*   76
JUDGMENT: *Judge Not Lest Ye Cast The First Stone
    Into Your Own Glass House*   78
JUSTICE: *The Last Piece Of Cake*   79

K

KARMA: *One Day You'll Pay, You'll All Pay*   84
KICKS: *If You Have Hair, Let It Down On Occasion*   86
KISMET: *Sometimes Fate Drops It In Our Laps*   87

L

LEGACY: *Last Bear In Marienbad -- A Post-Interview
    Addendum*   92
LOGIC: *How To Solve A Murder*   94
LOVE: *Are You In The Mood For It?*   96

M

MANNERS: *Why The MacPhersons Are No Longer Welcome
    In My Home*   100
MIRACLES: *In Praise Of The Wireless*   103
MYSTERY: *An Encounter Between Intimates*   105

N

NEMESIS: *An Enemy Is Just A Person Who Doesn't Like*   108
    You Very Much
NERVE: *Grow A Pair, Why Don't You?*   110
NOURISHMENT: *The Taste Of An Epicurean*   112

O

OBSCENITY: *I Don't Want To Alarm You*   116
OBSTINACY: *Stick It To Yourself*   119
OVERINDULGENCE: *It's Time For An Intervention*   120

P

PASSION: *Just Don't Frighten The Horses*   124
PREPAREDNESS: *Survival Of The Wittiest*   126
PRESENCE: *What You Give To The World*   128

Q

QUALIFICATIONS: *Have You Got A License For That?*   130
QUIETUDE: *I've Got Something To Say About Silence*   132
QUIRKS: *Yes, I Did That Deliberately*   135

R

RECOVERY: *Hair Of The Dog That Bit You*   138
RESOLUTION: *Everyday In Every Way*   140
RITES OF PASSAGE: *Darling Buds Of May*   142

S

SENSIBILITY: *Money And Shoes*   146
SPIRITUALITY: *A Spiritual Journey On The 11.55*   149
    To Carlisle
SUPPORT: *Mind Your Business*   151

T

TOLERANCE: *A Wild Garden Can Be A Lovely Garden*   154
TRADITION: *The Gee-Gees And Me*   156
TRUST: *No Raccoon Has Ever Lied To Me*   159

U

UGLINESS: *The Good Are Good—The Bad,*   164
     Frightfully Ugly
UNDERSTANDING: *Don't Say You Do If You Don't*   167
UPBRINGING: *Everything My Mother Did Was Wrong*   169

V

VERACITY: *I Rarely Sleep With Liars*   172
VIGILANCE: *Crime Prevention Tips*   175
VOICE: *Let No One Speak for You*   177

W

WISDOM: *Let's Just Have A Think About That*   180
WORK: *Work Makes You Many Things But Free*   183
     Isn't One of Them
WORDS: *On Keeping One's Head*   185

XYZ

YOUTH: *Hobbies, Not Just For Horses*   191
ZODIAC: *There Shall Be Signs in The Sun, And In*   194
     The Moon, And In The Stars

FINAL THOUGHTS

FOREWORD
Agatha, The Miss Behind The Myth

Agatha Whitt-Wellington (Miss) has had a long and luxurious career, moulding the world in which we live into a better shape (namely, a more hexagonal one). From humble beginnings in a modestly stinking rich family from Trenton, New Jersey, to the charming English village in which she has now taken residence, Miss Agatha has dedicated her life to improving the lives of others, primarily by improving her own and letting it serve as an example. By encouraging people to be more like herself (ie, better than they currently are), she hopes the world's populace will soon be able to sort some of these difficulties that blight the broadsheets every morning.

Her publications are too numerous to mention; her affairs too controversial to detail; her impact simply too astonishing to summarise in mere words. Miss Agatha has played a part in almost all aspects of recent history, sometimes by changing its course, sometimes by being a slightly interested bystander. Suffice it to say, she's important. That's the main thing you need to know.

With the helpful hand of Christopher, her Boy Friday, Agatha has collected her insights and made them available to you. But she's not just doing this for her health, you know, so please be aroused by the plenitude of wisdom, counsel and sexual escapades contained herein. This thoughtful tome, her alphabetical guide to appreciating life's ups and tackling its downs, should inspire all of us to improve ourselves and ultimately our world.

Strap yourself in, keep your motor running and savour the ride (which, coincidentally, is precisely what Miss Agatha said to me the first night we slept together).

Her devoted fan,
Rupert Stanley Quim
Publisher, *Specific Monthly*

A

ACCEPTANCE
Minds Are Like Parachutes -- Made Out Of Relatively Flimsy Material

I don't understand why many Americans are so uptight and inflexible. The same ones who claim to love America and its freedoms are often the ones who want the government to restrict others' expression of those freedoms. Freedom doesn't work like that, I'm afraid. Instead of trying to limit what others can do, say and feel, you should focus on yourself and try opening your mind a little rather than being so judgmental.

Now before you start assuming that I'm talking about sex, let me clarify that I am talking about sex. I'm guessing that your average Mr and Mrs American Pie would greatly object to a politician instructing them where, when and for how long to "make love." Maybe it's the Mr's birthday and he'd like to try the "tractor pull" he's been hearing the fellas at work talking about. Shouldn't he, presuming his wife's wearing kneepads, have the freedom to do this? But these couples are often the same ones who expect the government to make judgment calls on other types of practices. Just because you don't fancy something doesn't mean others shouldn't (see my cookbook *It Takes Balls To Eat This* for a food-related version of this statement).

There are even some mad fanatics who don't just want to legislate which organs people can rub against each other; they also want to make laws about which kinds of love are legitimate. As you know, I personally am no fan of marriage and would be more than happy for it to be banned permanently. But until it is, who should have the say about which marriages are right and which are wrong? My parents' marriage was "legal" but few (not even my father) see it as "right."

In fact, it seems to me that if you hate homosexuals so much, you'd jump at the chance to inflict upon them the tortures of marriage. Get your stories straight, straighties!

Many worry that as a country gets more open-minded, "alternative" practices will begin to be forced on everyone, and law and order as we know it will break down. If we let gays marry, they say, pretty soon it will be legal -- nay, obligatory -- for people to marry their pets. Now come on. When was the last time something worked like that?

Being open-minded means being secure with who you are and letting others do the same. I think Paul McCartney said it best when he sang, "Live and let die." Except for the second part, of course.

ADVICE
Do As I Say

As you know, I've been blessing readers, loved ones and strangers with tidbits of advice for most of my natural born life and I always love hearing from those who have followed my suggestions and bettered their lives in some way.

Alas, my work appears never to be done as every day I get messages (both via electronic mail and the proper way) which request more of my counsel. Although I do my best to answer each one personally (and I'm talking about really answering them, where I actually read them, think about the question and write out a response -- not that usual crap celebrities pull where they include some generic response card with a preprinted signature); however, I (in case you've forgotten) am only one woman (in case you've forgotten) and recently have fallen a bit behind in my correspondence. So I thought I'd take the opportunity to answer a few queries, in the hopes that if you yourself have a similar question, you'll find the answer you seek and won't bother me with it in future.

Help Agatha!
My mother–in–law is getting married next month, and I don't know what to buy her. Although her son and I have only been going together for two years, this is the fourth wedding of hers I've had to attend, and I've just run out of ideas. Any pointers?
Signed, Amanda

Dear Amanda,
Your mother-in-law is a whore and, as such, requires no additional gift to mark her next wedding. Trust me, she clearly is getting everything she needs already.
Yours, Agatha

Dear Miss Agatha,
I have a stubborn stain on one of my silk camisoles. As it was rather dear, I would like to know what I can use to clean it, without ruining the delicate material. Do you have any suggestions?
In anticipation, Mrs Charles Bris

Dear Mrs Bris,
I confess I must plead ignorance on this matter. Christopher does all my laundering and while I know he has the knowledge you are looking for (he's removed many a grass stain from my stockings' knees), I'm afraid he, having signed a confidentiality clause, is not at liberty to share this information.
Yours, Agatha

Dear Miss Whitt-Wellington,
I do not feel my boyfriend appreciates me. When I call him on the phone, he hangs up as soon as he hears my voice and he has refused to see me for almost eighteen months now. What can I do to strengthen his commitment to me?
Signed, Is It Me? in Ipswich

Dear Is It Me?,
Of course, it's not you. It's always them. All men in the world can be divided into two categories: the Spankys and the Alfalfas. Spankys are kind, gentle, and find no problem betraying their friends to make sure their women are safe and happy. Unfortunately, they are few and far between -- you may have more luck if you travel abroad; Spankys are thick and fast in France, where they are known by the charming name, *les homosexuels*. Alfalfas, on the other hand, are usually self-centred and thoughtless, wrapped up in their own little worlds without a care for their lady friend's needs or desires. I think you may have an Alfalfa on your hands, I'm afraid. It's usually not their fault they are like they are: generally they had some kind of issue with their mothers which caused their misogynistic tendencies. While

we can pity them, why on Earth should we pay because they were weaned off the tit too early? Alfalfas are good for one thing, which is ideal as they are usually quite skilled with their knobs, but after you get it, it's best to chuck them pronto.
Yours, Agatha

Agatha,
You are my last hope. I can find no pleasure in life. No matter how hard I try, everything seems to go wrong. Please tell me what to do.
If I don't hear from you in the next forty-eight hours, I intend to kill myself.
From Desperate in Dover

Dear Desperate,
Neat handwriting is ever so important to interpersonal relationship. Due to your sloppy penmanship and refusal to plump for a first class stamp, your letter has only now just reached me. Your other problems are no doubt not unrelated to your lack of care with your written communication. Chin up!
Yours, Agatha

CONFIDENTIAL to Worried Willy in Woking
The answer is eight inches, but until you learn to clean up that filthy mouth of yours, I think you'll find that your concern is purely academic.
PS. The next time you write, please hand deliver to my chamber. I keep the back door on the latch.

ART
Throwing Down Gang Signs For Dummies

A recent rash of graffiti in the village has stirred the fear of gang violence once again. While I try to have patience with those less fortunately gifted in the brain department, I confess this ignorance is really doing my head in.

Of course, real gang violence does exist, and I'd certainly file it in the "bad news" department. But the hysteria about gangs -- similar to what we've seen regarding Big Cats or hepatitis -- has got a bit out of control and needs to be reeled back in before we all look the fool and/or someone gets hurt (or hepatitis).

I can speak with authority on this topic because a number of years ago, I was in fact a member of a gang. It's a long and actually quite hilarious story; I've not got the time to share it with you at the moment except to say that I was not present when Chico slashed those gringos and I've proved that in court on two separate occasions. My experience, though, has given me insight into gang behaviour and has convinced me that my village can just settle itself down about the spray painting issue.

Symbolism is quite important to all groups of people, and gangs are no exception. Gang members, like yogis and deaf people, often use their hands to make signs that have meanings that outsiders do not understand. These can be seen in rap music videos and at schoolyards, skating rinks and other areas where young hoodlums frequent. Meanings can also be seen in written symbols, and in some cases, gang members do leave these marks in public places to "tag" or identify their territory. Individual gangs will develop their own marks, some of which seem nonsensical or random whereas others are actually quite logical (such as when a large "X" is used to represent The Spot). These symbols needn't be feared -- they're actually just chances for gang members to exercise their creativity, and in many cases, graffiti of this sort can be quite beautiful and beneficial to a community by making it more colourful and artistic.

I am not a snob when it comes to art, and you should not be either. When a man, woman or young person, picks up paint and lets it flow, we must look closely and appreciate its message: whether it's telling us about love, the nature of humanity or the fact that G-man is the Weed King. With a little bit of cultural knowledge, we can understand the world we see.

The saddest thing that we as a society can do is make judgments without the facts. And once again, let me reiterate, the facts show that I was in no way implicated in those murders so I'd appreciate not hearing anything more about it.

B

BEAUTY
The Gorgeousness Within

Those of you lucky enough to have been a visitor to one of my many splendid homes will know that my stairwells are lined with framed self-portraits of me which I myself have painted. While some may see this as a display of vanity, they would be wrong, and I will not even warrant their accusation with an explanation. My self-portraits are simply visual reminders of the exciting and enviable life of a beautiful and much-loved woman. Why people need to try to tarnish a sentiment as lovely as that with slurs is beyond my comprehension.

A darling family tradition in our household was that each of us, on the morning of our birthdays, created a self-portrait, in what ever medium we felt most accurately represented ourselves (though my mother frowned upon our making clay sculptures after my father's thirtieth birthday piece entitled "My Extremely Large Member: A Retrospective Over Three Decades"). Although my first two self-portraits were admittedly produced through a technique involving my mother forcing a marker pen into my small hand and gripping it tightly as she attempted to coerce me into drawing a smiley face on the canvas, I can still recall my first proper self-portrait on the morning of my third birthday. Imagine the excitement of waking to a rousing verse of "For She's a Jolly Good Fellow" and being led downstairs to a quick breakfast of *Oeufs à la Cantalienne* before having the ceremonial smock placed over my head and the coloured pencil case laid opened before me. I remember that I paused, closed my eyes and really carefully considered all that had gone on in my life that year before determinedly beginning to sketch the rough outlines of three-year-old Miss Agatha Whitt-Wellington.

Alas, I was not blessed with enough talent as an artist to "make it" in that competitive and cut-throat world. Yet I have remained devoted to the tradition, having had my most recent masterpiece expertly hung by Christopher just last month and a fine addition to the gallery it is. Even the men who laid my carpeting (who couldn't be expected to appreciate such exquisite creativity) commented on my artwork and were awestruck to find that I am both the model and artiste.

We all need more beauty in our lives, and we certainly aren't going to get it in from the likes of Damien Hirst, the Chapman Brothers and the rest of that lot of artistic charlatans. Where better to find that beauty than within ourselves? I encourage you to go have a good look in the mirror right now. Study your face -- even those of you who acknowledge that others find your appearance hideous, please do your best to look past your grotesque features and focus on the way your eyes reveal your inner soul and your mouth speaks of experience. Then go create. Let your inner fire take you and put your face on paper like you've never done before!

One last practical note: in these times of financial strife, copies of your self-portrait, professionally framed, make thoughtful and relatively inexpensive gifts. I cannot begin to describe the look of incredulity that has spread over the faces of my friends and admirers when they've been presented with reproductions of my self-portraits (particularly selections from the nude series I did in my twenties). I will never forget how my grandfather's jaw dropped!

BELONGING
My Cobbled Road To Damascus

I don't pledge my allegiance to just anyone, you know. Ever since the debacle which found me serving as President of the Mile High Club for a few months in 1989, I have been determined to thoroughly investigate any organization before signing up. After living in Britain for a while, I was given the opportunity to become a citizen. Before I submitted my application, I knew I should do some research.

As a keen bibliophile, I am a firm supporter of public libraries, particularly my local branch as it still has one of those gorgeous old oak card catalogs. Of course, it's completely useless as a tool for finding books, so patrons have to rely on the staff's photographic memory of every single shelf in the building. On the first day of my research, I met the head librarian, a charming, bespectacled chap called Sherlock Tellerman. I explained that I was hoping to understand Britain -- its history, government, customs and culture -- and needed it all wrapped up within four days as I was dashing off that weekend to give a lecture on my series of novels set at a women's college in Ho-Ho-Kus, New Jersey. Mr Tellerman led me to a darkened room, where I spent the rest of the afternoon, combing through dusty tomes.

Despite the fact that I hail from the US, a young country still holding onto its girlish figure, history is extremely important to me. Though I had had some knowledge of British history, of course -- I'm not an idiot and don't like your implication that I am -- I was amazed by the tales I found in those books. That room literally stank of time immemorial. And while I do not support violence, I must commend the various kings and queens for practicing their violence with such gusto. You've got to have a reluctant admiration for a king who loved animals so much that he executed his own son for looking at a chicken in a dastardly manner (as King Dingelbert did). Now I'm as red-white-and-blue as the next person, but let's face it, America's got nothing on England when it comes to history.

I also was enthralled by the rich culture of which the books spoke. I pored through the pages of wonderful literature; photographs of art, statues and photographs; and biographies of musicians and dancers. I hate to confess this, but I was previously unaware that it was a Brit who first discovered that applying oil paint to canvas rather than directly into one's eyes allows for a more enjoyable and less blindingly painful experience of art. How different the optometry world would have been without him!

Although I was impressed with the majority of what I had read, I was still hesitant; it had always been my policy to back a winning team. I enjoyed living in the UK, but should I hitch my wagon in such an intimate way to a country whose star, many argued, was on the wane?

The following day as I was leaving the building, Mr Tellerman stopped me to check on my progress. I lauded his text recommendations, but apparently his lifelong work in a silent library had heightened his sensitivity to apprehension in a woman's voice. He generously invited me to join him for a cup of tea and offered to fill in any gaps in my education (this is not a euphemism). I never pass up a chance to get inside a man's head (again, not a euphemism), so I agreed to accompany him to his flat for a cuppa, a biscuit and first-hand evidence (euphemism) of why I should become British.

Sherl's home was a mix of met expectations and intriguing surprises. The walls were lined with shelves of books and newspapers, yet I noticed that there seemed to be no rhyme or reason -- Shakespeare sat next to Foucault and a few texts were displayed backwards or upside down. What was up with that? There was a piano squeezed into one room, though he claimed he did not play. The bedroom ceiling was cracked and stained yet, I later found out, it was decorated with glow-in-the-dark star-shaped details. I was captivated by the man's mystery.

The visit began with the librarian's retelling of his own biography. As an experienced member of the literati, I couldn't help being bored by his childhood stories (early death of mother, verbal abuse by father, bullying at school, blah blah blah), but things finally picked up when he began explaining how his Britishness influenced his life as a man. His understanding of his nation's past inspired him to look toward its future and the role he would play in it. Perhaps the tea (did I mention that he filled the pot with an equal measure of whiskey?) had loosened his inhibition, but he ended his tale with the proposal that Britain's future was now playing a key role in his own life by being the sole reason that his and my paths had crossed.

Needless to say, this comment quickly led to the removal of our clothes and a stumbling to his private chamber (my desire to politely accept compliments is not unrelated to my desire to get laid). It was here, ultimately, that I solidified my decision. A country that could arouse such devotion to cause an intelligent man to call out "God Save the Queen" at climax, well, that was a country I wanted to be a part of.

The day I officially converted, Sherl was by my side. It was quite a moving experience with a brief talk on the historical importance of our county, a round of applause after the official welcome and a beautiful rendition by a local school's orchestra of the National Anthem (though I confess I sang the words to "My Country, 'Tis of Thee" in my head). My bookish companion then took me for a walk through a museum, a fish and chip dinner and a quick shag in the backroom of a working man's club -- the most British of British evenings out.

Sadly, my commitment to my new country ultimately surpassed my commitment to my new paramour (his habit of over-sugaring the tea quickly became intolerable). But I often look back fondly on that brief encounter which played such an important part of making me the woman I now I am -- part American, part British and completely certain that the men who sit in silence all day are the noisiest in the sack.

BETRAYAL
Separating The Lights From The Dark

As we've just entered the final month of the year, I presume most of us are in the holiday spirit, except those who are not celebrating upcoming holidays, but there seems to be so many festivals these days that I don't really know who those who aren't celebrating may be, so I feel it is probably safe to assume that we are celebrating, okay, let's not quibble over the details, shall we? Now that we've established that we're all in the holiday spirit, I would like to explain what happened to me this evening, because I feel it is an excellent example of how the holiday spirit can be used to overcome even the greatest of woes.

For the past eight seasons, I have been asked to switch on the lights in our village. It's always been a modest affair; we're a small village and naturally I am seen as our most relevant citizen. I don't like to disappoint, so Christopher has always driven me down to the Green on the special night -- I get out, switch on the lights, wave to a few children, watch the Vicar attempt to persuade a melody out of the rather feeble but extremely willing choir and then head home for a wash and a nightcap before retiring for the evening. Job done. This is how it has always been, and I have yet to hear a single complaint voiced from anyone.

This year, I assumed, would be the same. The fact that I had not received a call from the head of the Village Green Christmas Lights Committee did not concern me in the least; after all, I am a busy woman and my phone is often engaged due to transatlantic requests for interviews and Christopher's newly discovered addiction to the Home Shopping Channel. So this evening I put on my coat and scarf, and Christopher and I headed into the village.

The sight which greeted us was diabolical. The village was

packed with motorcars; even the handicapped spaces in front of Scope were full. I really do not understand why people insist on driving their cars around a village as small as ours. Haven't they an inkling about the size of their carbon footprints? Nonetheless, Christopher dropped me at the Green, agreeing to circle until the deed was done.

Although I am a public figure who has had to grow used to them, crowds have never been my favourite, but I made it through to the makeshift grandstand to locate Mr Whitehall, the committee chairman. When our eyes met, I knew instantly that trouble was afoot.

"Dear Miss Agatha," he claimed in a voice I know recognize as a weasel's (if weasels had voices). "Why, we weren't expecting you."

I am happy to say that my reply was "You know I'd never let my community down."

I was soon to discover that my community, alas, did not feel the same way about me. It came to pass that I had been replaced as the turner-oner of the Christmas lights. As simple as that. Instead the honour was being given to small armless child from eight miles away who, in early October, despite his lack of arms, had managed to ring 999 when his mother fell down a flight of stairs. The Committee had voted last week to invite this young boy to turn on the lights and had even rigged up a system which would allow him to do it with his nose (which he apparently had also used to dial Emergency Services).

This is all well and good. I have nothing against this deformed lad, and I'm sure his mother, despite her disappointment at having a freak for a child, was grateful for his quick thinking and sturdy proboscis. My beef is not with him.

It is with the Committee. For I know the real reason I was

replaced this year, and it had nothing to do with Little Lawrence's heroism. I was replaced due to a disagreement I had with Winnie Whitehall at this summer's fete over the judging in the Bakewell tart competition. I am not saying my tart was the best in the competition, but I am saying that Winnie had no business being a judge in that division. I found this to be a travesty and contacted a good friend at a national newspaper, who wrote a rather damning article about the way this mainstay of English life has been corrupted by unfair and brutal judges.

And that is why I was passed over. However, this is not a piece about the pettiness of the members of the VGCL Committee, who by the by are mostly ugly and whose gardens are substandard. It is a piece about the triumph of the holiday spirit so I shall continue.

I admit I was initially shaken by this public shunning, but I immediately remembered my holiday spirit and went straight up to Lawrence to congratulate him on being chosen. I did not even shy away when, instead of extending his hand which he had none of, he put out his small boot for me to shake. That is how polite I was despite the rudeness shown to me by the Committee. After shaking his boot, I then approached his mother. I gave her a copy of my most recent book (which I always carry with me for situations just like this), and I even signed the plaster cast on her arm (which was the same as giving her fifty pounds really since that's the going rate for my autograph, and I'm sure she can sell that when she's healed). I then walked to the edge of the Green where Christopher picked me up, and we went home. I presume the lights came on without undue problems, and the whole sordid affair is now behind me.

That is how the holiday spirit can triumph over evil.

C

CLARITY
Memo To All Idiots -- Stop Being Idiots

This morning, a friend sent me an email letter to which was attached a photograph of something she saw on her travels across the US (I won't say which state it was in, but if you assume it was a Midwestern one, you would not be wrong). It was of a bumper sticker that read:

> If I pass you on the right,
> your in the wrong.

The car displaying this sticker was unsurprisingly red and had hubcaps on its wheels which spun even when the vehicle was stationary.

Unlike in England where roads are so narrow bicyclists can barely fit down them, most roads in America are multi-laned in each direction. Americans drive on the right side of the road (and before any Britons assume that I mean right as in correct, rest assured I mean right as in not left: you will not find me in any motoring-based morality arguments like that). The general guideline is that those driving the speed limit should drive in the right lane, and that the left lane be used only by those who are speeding (which happily makes it quite easy for coppers to spot lawbreakers). The left lane therefore is also known (by twats) as the "fast lane."

Clearly the driver in the red Ford displaying said bumper sticker feels strongly about this guideline. He is so obviously outraged by those in the left lane traveling at the speed limit that not only does he feel the need to overtake them, he also takes the opportunity to remind them that they are in fact "wrong." I can only deduce from his placing of a non-removable decal on his vehicle (not even on the bumper, mind, but across the rear window) that the "fast lane" issue is a passion of his, something he feels in the very pit of his soul.

Perhaps I should admire his commitment. However, I do not. Because he is clearly an idiot, and idiots do not deserve admiration for anything they do. There is one simple clue to his idiocy -- though I've no doubt there's plenty more evidence available -- and I trust that you all spotted it instantly within my unbiased description above.

It's the word your.

Not driving fast in the "fast lane" may be frustrating and naive, but if you need a great example of something that is across-the-board, out-and-out wrong, you need look no further than the word your.

Your means "belonging to you." I assume the driver meant you're, as in "you are" in the wrong. While I acknowledge the two words sound the same, they are in fact two completely different words. The bumper sticker might as well as read "tomato in the wrong." Tomato does not mean you're and your does not mean you're.

God gave us the English language to use to communicate with one another. It's a great language. It's got words like crumbly and delicate and trumpery, fantastic words that incorporate a range of sounds and many shades of meaning. But the language only works when used correctly. Using words incorrectly destroys marriages (my darling, our love is so holey) or results in incarceration (I have the head of that old dear hanging over my fireplace). Using words incorrectly is wrong.

If I ran the world (which as of yet, I do not), people driving slowly in the left lane wouldn't give me much pause. But people who say your when they mean you're would immediately be banished to Idiot Island (formerly Molokai) where they would be exiled until they learned to speak correctly. If that took their entire lifetimes, then so be it.

COMPANIONSHIP
My Relationship With The Lesser Species

I am an animal lover. From the time I was but a wee one, I have almost always had an animal companion by my side. My first pet was a traditional one; he was a stray dog whom we originally met when we discovered he was operating a betting shop from inside our garage. While we admired both his resourcefulness and creativity, this was no life for a dog and we set out to reform him. I loved little Brown Leonard (as we named him) and still recall fondly our walks around the esplanades of Trenton, NJ. He was always up for an adventure or a game of cards. Our relationship was based upon mutual respect, unconditional love and a substantial amount of gambling debt.

Of course, while I was still a child, my parents, or rather my father, selected our pets. In our household, my parents shared responsibility: my mother controlled everything and my father did what he was told. As my mother felt our reputation in the neighbourhood had suffered as a result of Brown Leonard's nefarious former livelihood, she assigned all future pet duties to my father. Throughout my tenure there, we shared our home with quite a menagerie. My father was particularly fond of fish, though his aquarium was positioned in his private study which no one but he could enter. Over the years, that collection of fish became a tropical smorgasbord of exotic varieties, recognised state-wide as a perfect mini eco-system and the only real friends my father had.

The story I shall now recount involves the first pet I chose on my own. I say chose but, of course, the philotherians amongst you will know that a pet actually chooses you. Before I began travelling the world, I was based in a darling flat in Camden, New Jersey where I was known as "the Lovely Lady" to the locals I refused to meet eyes with on the street. It's lonely when you leave a house full of love, liquor and noise, so I deduced that a pet might ease that pain. Unfortunately, most of the animals at the local shelter had backgrounds which I felt were too dissimilar from my own. But one afternoon I returned home to see find a small, rather trampish looking dog asleep on my doorstep. As I unlocked the door, he rushed in, climbed upon my settee and went back to sleep. Although this type of behaviour would be abhorrent from a human (yes, I am referring to Captain Snezley during his troubled years), I found it almost endearing from this pup. Through research, I discovered that his breed was most likely Telomian, and I felt that he and I understood that a better life was deserved by both of us. I named him Sebastian and felt satisfied I had found my new best friend.

Sebastian slept soundly for the first three days post-arrival while I purchased a large array of items to make his new home comfortable. When he first began to investigate his new surroundings, though, he showed little interest in the toys, chews and reading materials I had selected for him. He instead preferred to stay crouched in the corner, occasionally peeping through the net curtains of the dining room window, watching closely the street. Having never been a dog myself, I was reticent to suggest alternative activities for him. I still considered him a friend but was beginning to doubt that he felt the same way towards me.

One afternoon (I remember it was a Tuesday, the day that unemployment checks were handed out so thankfully few of my neighbours were congregating on my street corner as they otherwise so charmingly did), a young policeman arrived at my door. As soon as the bell went, Sebastian ran upstairs in a way that made me feel he did not want to be seen. I permitted the officer to enter my house and, after pouring him a cup of tea, I asked him to sit with me in the sitting room. He looked tired, and I inquired about the case that was clearly exhausting him so. Here he began a tale of such criminality that I shall spare you the details (which I don't remember). But suffice it say, I felt victimised just hearing them. Before I could offer my advice on the best course of action in solving this conundrum, the young officer produced from his pocket a photograph (shoddily taken but clear enough to recognise) of Sebastian. I immediately put on a brave face. He asked if I had seen this creature, lurking. Although I normally try to keep my responses to police officers' questions as close to the truth as possible, I confess in this circumstance I told a falsehood. He then bid me adieu, leaving his calling card in the basket near the door, put there for that very purpose.

Needless to say, I instantly confronted Sebastian about his involvement with illegal activities. He denied everything. I wanted to believe him and I told him I did, but I still had my suspicions. We lived together for another week but by then we had become strangers. Although it broke my heart to pieces, I spoke to the boy next door and arranged for Sebastian to be shot and removed from the premises while I was at the market.

The house no longer seemed the same. It was now free of his masterful criminal mind, but it also lacked that love which can only exist between man and beast. Despite what had passed between us, I never grassed up Sebastian to the police. The guilt clearly had made him suffer enough. I missed him, but as I was by then planning my first trip to Europe and a pet would have complicated my itinerary, I believe the situation's resolution was probably the best for both of us.

Relationships with animals are magical and in many ways more rewarding than most of the interactions I've had with fellow humans. I suppose the lesson here is that, no matter how good you are, how loving you are, you cannot trust anyone with a blue tongue. Keep this in mind, young ones, particularly when out and about on the dating scene.

COURTSHIP
Dreams And Worship In The Summer Sun

As the weather seems to be turning to summer time all over the world (except in places where it is not), I have been seeing more and more youngsters in their cricket whites roaming the streets, bats in hand. Even as I dictate this, I can hear the swift thwack of willow as I watch three boys pummeling a car across the road, in what I presume is one of our local eleven's pre-match rituals. Well done, lads -- with batting like that, we'll be guaranteed a win!

I am rather partial to cricket, partly because it reminds me of baseball, an American game I loved as a child. Cricket and baseball share many similarities: balls and bats are used, they each have a fair amount of running and hitting, umpires are present and everyone, save the most refined of minds, finds them both excruciatingly tedious.

Despite my love of the American pastime, it was at a baseball field that my heart was first broken. It may surprise some of you to find out that I was quite a sportswoman in my youth. My family has always believed that -- in addition to being well-respected, wealthy and famous -- being well-rounded is also essential. Therefore I tried my hand at a number of athletic endeavours. During the summer of my first heartbreak, my main role was as shortstop for the Trenton Lady Tigers. (I do love how simply placing the word "Lady" in front of a team's nickname makes the whole concept seem that much more sophisticated.) We practised every weekday evening, and our games were held on Saturday afternoons. I declined the offer of captaincy as I felt it was important to give other, less confident girls a go, but your assumption that I was the glue which held the team together is far from incorrect.

Our season was progressing quite well; we managed to defeat all opposition without much perspiration. In addition to my defensive skills, I was a bit of a star hitter and was, unbeknownst to me, gathering quite a following amongst the boys of our neighbourhood. I had always been rather popular with the opposite sex, but it was this summer where my nickname "The Swinger" really took hold. One particular youth, a freckled-faced teen named Darren, became my number one fan. He would come to games with handwritten signs of support, which bore slogans such as "Go All the Way with Aggie!" and "Love the Way Aggie Handles Balls" and were illustrated with quite life-like sketches of me in various positions of exertion. (After serving a short time in prison in his twenties, Darren actually went on to become a highly regarded watercolourist, with shows in galleries throughout New England.) Over the weeks as I continued to be drawn by Darren, I realised I was also becoming drawn to Darren, but it wasn't until the playoffs that I finally managed to have a private word with him.

The night of our first round triumph, Darren and I had a somewhat intense meeting in the backseat of his car and when we emerged, it was clear to all who were watching that we were now in love. I anticipated that my new found relationship would do nothing but strengthen my athleticism and that the remainder of the playoffs would go off without a hitch. How wrong I was. In our next game, I dropped two flies and did little else to improve my stats. In the field, I could not focus on the game and, at bat, my wrist action was appalling. Through the grace of God, we managed to come out on top. I knew then and there that I had to stop seeing Darren until after the final game.

While I expected that he would be upset -- after all anyone denied my favours even for a few short days is bound to be saddened -- I did not expect him to take the hard line. He told me quite simply that it was either baseball or him. If I continued to play, I was not only no longer welcome in the backseat of his car but a quick blowy in the alley was also out of the question. I was gobsmacked. I had to then choose between the glory of victory and the wonderful but fleeting pleasures of the flesh, by which, of course, I mean the truest of love.

I don't mind telling you the decision was a difficult one. Darren did his best to persuade me over the next week (once three times in one night) but by the following Saturday morning, I knew my duty was to my teammates. After all they (unlike Darren) could not achieve the ultimate climax without me.

At two o'clock, I suited up and walked on to the field. I kept it together until the seventh inning stretch when I heard Darren's Buick backfire from behind the stands. I tried to stay focused on the game, but my heart was visibly breaking through my number twenty-seven jersey. Both teams managed three up, three down so that at the bottom of the ninth, the scores were level and I was on deck. It was at this point that Darren emerged from his car, holding a sign emblazoned with the words "Agatha the Swinger goes down today." I was instantly cheered -- he would take me back after the game! Needless to say, I scored the winning run and after my lap of honour, I ran over to Darren, expecting a welcome embrace and a kiss of congratulations. Unfortunately I had misread the message of his poster, and he explained that its intent was actually to jinx me. He turned from me, grabbed at the breast of our leftfielder and walked out of my life forever.

Despite this incident, my love of baseball has not diminished. Although I no longer play, you'll often find me humming "Take Me Out to the Ballgame" as I prick out my Sweet Williams and tend to the Morning Glories.

Fortunately, in England, it is against the law for women to participate in cricket matches, so while I have taken a few good lengths after a full toss in the locker rooms at Edgbaston, I have never had to choose between the sport and a relationship.

I bid you adieu now as I'll be heading over to the pavillion just as soon as I answer a few questions from the lovely constable who has just rung my bell.

Whether you be a player or a spectator, enjoy the summer sun, play everything with a straight bat and keep your balls well polished!

D

DIPLOMACY
Cruel To Be Kind

My dear friend Alice Wintergarden seems to have gotten herself in a pickle again. She really does have a knack for that, which is both charming and maddening as her pickles always seem to correspond with needing something from me at a time when I just don't have much energy left to give (yes, dear readers, I am not perfect). However, once again I came to her rescue, despite the fact it meant that I was unable to listen to a radio programme to which I was looking forward all week. Why must I always be the good friend? I suppose it's my curse.

Alice spends each Thursday afternoon at our local library. She calls it her "me time" and claims that she uses the hours to look at the newspapers, read aloud to the children's group and peruse the biography section. However, Christopher (who has occasionally witnessed Alice in action) tells me that what she is actually doing is what his mates call "cruising."

Now, as you know, I'm not one to sit in judgment of anyone's choices, and certainly not the choices of a dear friend whose poor taste in lovers has left her bereft of gentlemanly company. More power to her, I say. However, participating in this kind of activity can have its consequences and had led to the pickle in which Alice now finds herself within.

What it boils down to is this: she has caught the favour of a certain man about whom she says she would rather kill herself than sleep with. Apparently this man is a nice enough sort, and she doesn't wish to hurt his feelings in any way. But she definitely does not want to sleep with him (nor does she want to kill herself), and it is over this that she has been crying at my kitchen table for the past few hours.

Per usual, my advice was thoughtful, correct and succinct: shut the fucker down.

So many of us are taught that other people's feelings matter and far be it from me to suggest that they don't (but they don't). The truth is that when we try to "spare another's feelings," we rarely do so. Instead, we drag it out, making things better for neither party. When we delay being honest in an effort to be kind, we risk one of two things: being weaseled into doing something we don't want to do or hurting the other party even more.

Let's examine those two options more closely. When I was younger, I briefly went through a stage, as most teenagers do, when I thought "Sod my parents' millions, I want to make it on my own." I therefore sought employ with a telemarketing agency (I had a seductive telephone voice even as a youth). The first rule we learned was: keep them talking. The longer we could keep a person talking, no matter how politely they were rejecting our sales pitch, the easier it would be to finally reel them in. If Alice were to sit down with this man and try to soften her rejection with a drawn out explanation, I don't doubt her evening would end with the dreaded walk of shame. Sadly, I say this out of personal experience. Even clever people like my good self can be talked into changing our minds after a while. If only I had heeded my own advice, I could have avoided that Maryland jail time for Unnatural or Perverted Sexual Practices. I guess sometimes we've got to learn the very hard way.

Besides, slowly breaking things off will actually make it a thousand times worse for the other person. No one needs to be rejected over and over, even if it's done in a kind voice. How many times must a person hear "I would rather eat glass than go to bed with you" before they finally just step in front of the #3808 at Trenton Transit Center? The answer is surprisingly few, I found out to my dismay (rest in peace, Homeless Tim). Sugarcoating a rejection is like sugarcoating cyanide: they're equally destructive but at least cyanide kills within seconds. Injuries from being hit by a train may lead a person to linger at death's door for weeks.

If we've learned nothing else from Jerry Springer, he's at least taught us that putting one's hand up to someone's face and simply saying no is the cleanest way to break off a relationship. Yes, there may be some shouting and a few chairs broken over the audience's heads, but it is still the quickest and most morally correct way to deal with the situation.

DISTINCTION
There's You And Then There's Me

I have style. I do. I can't tell you how many times young women have complimented my beautiful dresses and men have slid their hands up my thigh to appreciate the silk of my stockings. I suppose I'm confessing to being a fashion plate, though I'm not totally comfortable with that role. I've never been a slave to fashion and find those who are happy to wear those chains (simply because those chains are "in vogue" this season) an embarrassment. Whatever Mary-Kate and/or Ashley may tell you, "the fashion world" is not about expressing oneself, celebrating women or turning the human body into a piece of art. It's about a small group of small people abusing the stupidity of those with cash and inferiority complexes. I'm not going to let fashion designers be the boss of me. I don't recommend you do so either. The truth is that those in the fashion world don't care about you, what you wear or how you feel about yourself. The other truth is that I don't really either.

For those of you who aspire to look like me, I'm afraid that you'll find no helpful hints here. I look good, not because of my extraordinary physique, my perfectly fitted clothing or my exquisite taste in jewellery. I look gorgeous because I've got that something special, that *je ne sais quoi* that is simply not available from the pages of a magazine or the racks of a trendy boutique.

There is a surprisingly simple test that will determine if you are in possession of this mysterious quality. Go to the fruit department of your nearest supermarket (chains stores only -- this is the one and only time it's acceptable not to support your local food grower). In full view of a shopworker of the opposite gender (regardless of which way you swing), take a piece of fruit and put it into your mouth. Women should go for a banana; men please choose a peach. If you can eat the entire thing without the shopkeeper stopping you, you have It. If you end up banned from the shop or with your photo in the local paper, you don't.

If you are lucky to have a mystique similar to mine, you should trust that not only do you look good, you will be invited to all the most interesting parties and probably have already been receiving the "beautiful people" discount, the existence of which may appear to be an urban myth but think about it: what decent prostitute would have charged an average person what she charged you? I take off my striking and ravishing hat to you. Welcome to the club.

If you don't have it, well, I'm afraid you're screwed. You can adorn your body with the most beautiful of fabrics, choose the most fabulous of perfume or shine your shoes to the perfect sheen, but if you ain't got It, you just ain't got It.

I'm sure you have other good qualities, somewhere deep down inside, but in all honesty, we beautiful people are wise to you -- your lack of It stinks up the street. Best of luck to you, my unfortunate friend. I'm afraid you've going to need it.

DUALITY
Perpetually An Expatriate

Coming back to the US for a visit has reminded me that, while I am at home in both the US and UK, I am also an expat in both countries. This is a precarious position to be in, though fortunately I am culturally flexible enough to maintain it.

Expat communities are delightful because they remind you of the people, places and ideas you left behind without actually forcing you to physically interact on a daily basis with those people, places and ideas. For example, in May I met an American gentleman at a wine tasting party I attended in St Ann's, Nottingham, and it was nice to spend the evening discussing topics which were of little interest to our English friends.

Perhaps the most extreme expat experience I've encountered happened a few years ago when I was asked to give the commencement speech at a high school in my hometown of Trenton, New Jersey. Two days before graduation, I was given a tour of the school (I must comment here about how delightfully polite the student council members who gave the tour were and how flattered I was when they named a section of their library the Whitt-Wellington Center for Underachievers). I was introduced to much of the student body, including many of the senior athletes; I confess I was pleasantly surprised to see how both intellectually and physically well-developed the boys were and I spent a full hour lingering in their locker room, discussing their futures and offering support where I could. I was then taken into individual classrooms where I could answer any questions the students or teachers had about my fascinating life. It was in the physics wing of the school where I met Mr Parkinson, who had only recently emigrated to New Jersey from Sunderland. He continually interrupted the many clever questions from his students I was attempting to field to ask about my experiences with Morris dancing. It soon became clear that our dear Mr

Parkinson was less interested in finding out about my own life and more interested in telling me about his. About twenty minutes in, he actually excused the students from the classroom (goodness knows what they got up to and how their parents felt about their being denied thirty minutes of physics tuition that day), locked the door and proceeded to demonstrate his personal Morris dancing technique before me (sadly, I am not speaking euphemistically). I was literally locked in a small room with a mad Morris dancing Mackem, wanting to be supportive while admittedly feeling a little more than anxious that the mace I was carrying in my handbag would soon be in use. Luckily his display ended before anyone's eyes got sprayed, and I immediately headed to the principal's office to complain. I believe Mr Parkinson was let go from the school shortly thereafter, but I was glad I could offer him my expat friendship for the brief duration of our acquaintance.

Of course, wherever you are in the world, you can find your own place and a sense of home. But my heart is always warmed when I bump into those who can appreciate parts of my past. It's good to meet someone who recognises the brand of sweets you used to eat when you were a child, the history of a team you grew up supporting or the particular hurtful and borderline racist remarks bandied about by the gangs in your city.

There's a great saying that goes, "There's no place like home." At the same time, we must remember that "home is where you hang your hat." In fact there are a number of sayings about home. Now that I think about it, I'm not sure any one of them really makes an ounce of sense.

E

ELOQUENCE
Wise Words From A Dead Man

My mother was on the blower this morning to inform me of the death of Mr Heron Williard, and to ask me if I wanted write something for his funeral.

Once she reminded me who the hell he was, I naturally agreed to do my best to whip something up.

For most of my youth, Mr Williard lived two houses down from ours, yet he always maintained a sense of mystery. I assume this is because the only thing he hated more than children was girl children, so basically he and I were never very close. I can only remember him ever saying three things to me, yet those wise words have stayed with me until this very day:

> 1. Give it more choke
> 2. If you're waiting for the postman, you just missed him
> 3. Don't be a wise guy

There's no way to ever really estimate the impact one person's life has made on this Earth, so it doesn't seem very prudent of me to try.

Rest in peace.

ENCOURAGEMENT
Inspiration And Sage Advice For Budding Scribes

I am often asked for tips on "making it in the writing biz." I am always, of course, too happy to offer inspiration and help to those readers who see me as their hero.

Unfortunately, though, becoming a good writer is quite honestly not really something the average person can do. Good writers are born, not made. So my first tip to would-be authors is to ensure that your ancestors' breeding stock is of the highest calibre, that your inheritance is substantial and that your family name alone will guarantee that publishers will fall over themselves to take a look at your work.

Once you've done that, the sky is your oyster. You will need to write, write, write. If you want this to be your vocation, you must commit to actually doing it. A cobbler spends eight hours a day cobbling, a writer must do the same. The profession is called writing for a reason so be prepared to write until you are blue in the hands. Even with my huge back catalog, I still pull my chair up to the desk and watch Christopher type for as many hours a day as I've had hot dinners. I do this without complaint: I accept that, as a wordsmith, this is my cross to bear.

Assuming you have already studied my own books, I suggest that you not really waste more time in reading others'. Most of what is published today is shite, and writers don't have the time to be dealing in shite. Be aware of the classics, of course, so that you can participate fully in literary conversations. But don't let anyone influence you. Doing so is in the most questionable taste. Just this morning when I opened my post, I found a request for my criticism on the work of twenty-year-old poet. I turned the page to see a sonnet beginning "My mistress' eyes are like a cinnamon bun" and immediately stopped reading. Above everything, you must be original or you will be destined for the bin, where I confess that poem now resides.

Finally, I've no doubt many a fool has already suggested that you "write what you know." Though pithy, this recommendation is worthless. Please take a moment to consider: look around your room, look at yourself in the mirror, look at the faces of your friends and family. My guess is that after this quick assessment of your life, you'll realise that "what you know" is hardly worth knowing, let alone writing or reading about. A writer must be honest, and I am trying to be honest with you now. Your life is boring and would not make a good book. Don't be fooled by encouraging spouses, supportive friends or doctors unwilling to diagnose you as delusional.

Writing is a ruthless business so prepare yourself for rejection. Even I myself have had pieces rejected, and it is difficult. There's no denying that. But if you are as dedicated and as talented a writer as possible, you just may find success. It can happen. And if it doesn't, there are other things out there for you, I am sure.

Life is a journey, and we must all make our own paths. If writing is the path for you, trust the process and your talent will clear the way of potholes, stray tacks and rodent carcasses. If it turns out that your path is not creative, don't fear, for we will all end up dead and alone eventually, darlings.

Now get to work!

ETIQUETTE
A Packet Of Crisps And A Pint Of Winkles

Like many of you I'm sure, this morning I was required to go visit a friend in hospital. Alice Wintergarden, whom you've heard me talk of on numerous occasions, is convalescing quietly after a "procedure," the details of which I have the decency to not publicly embarrass her about.

Unlike many of you I'm sure, I don't hate visiting people in hospital. This is because I am aware of the proper etiquette that must accompany any excursion to an infirmary. Sadly, many people are ignorant of these guidelines. This not only causes them to find their visits unpleasant, but also affects me personally by requiring me to have to fill out tedious complaint forms. So I shall enlighten you all at this time.

1. *Dress Code*
It's important to "look the part" of a concerned visitor. Men must sport ties. Women should not wear trousers. Call me outdated, but the truth is that the sight of a woman's pins can actually be restorative to the poorly gentlemen in the wards. It's a medical fact (it's something to do with the shape of the calf). A quick note about stockings: because nurses wear black (in the UK) or white (in the US), lady visitors should avoid these colours. Fishnets are also never appropriate.

Additionally, regardless of one's gender, make sure you have a handkerchief about your person. Hospitals are warm places (better for the breeding of bacteria) and while a hint of perspiration can give one that recently-sated glow, if a drip appears, it must be instantly wiped away.

2. *Thoughtful Gifts*
It used to be that hospital visitors always arrived laden down with flowers or chocolates. Unfortunately, people seem to have

developed allergies to almost everything these days (flowers, plants, perfume, work, etc) so a bouquet and chocolates (which seem to always contain nuts even when they don't contain nuts) could get you into a bind.

The intention behind both of these gifts -- to cheer the poor sods -- is good, though. Flowers brighten up the place and chocolates serve as a "treat" to counteract the universally acknowledged "trick" of horrid hospital food. The problem with this theory, however, is the very logic behind it. Hospitals are full of nurses who generally are dour (wouldn't you be if you had to see what they have to see) as well as extremely lonely (undoubtedly connected to their choice of stocking colour -- see above), and therefore nursing staff are incredibly tempted to take (and by take, I mean steal) any lovely presents that are carried in (especially those given to patients who are comatose -- nurses see this as a "victimless crime").

Therefore, you must find a balance between a gift that your friend will enjoy and one which isn't too seductive to medical personnel. Or you may want to consider taking two gifts in: one for the sickly and one for his or her caretaker. A good suggestion is one of my books -- all people, regardless of their health, enjoy them, and doing so doubles my profits. Everyone wins!

3. *Topics Of Conversation*
Many visitors ask patients about their health. This is a mistake. Think about it: their health is all these people have been talking about during their hospital stay, they must be sick of it by now. (Ignore or admire the pun.) Therefore, you should talk about the exact opposite topic: your health. I've yet to visit anyone who wasn't fascinated hearing about how well I am feeling.

Some people imagine that those in hospital would like to hear about the "outside" world. This is a fallacy. If a person were interested in anything outside of themselves, they wouldn't have gotten sick and ended up in hospital in the first place.

4. *Length Of Stay*

No one is required to stay for the entire length of visiting hours. To be polite, the minimum length of a visit should be a maximum of four minutes. Other than that, you can leave whenever you want. You've done a good deed just by showing up at all, don't forget. To combat any awkwardness, end all visits by insisting you must dash because you've promised to visit a sick child in the kiddie ward. No one will insist you stay if they think they are keeping you from Little Tommy Failingliver.

Visiting the sick is certainly no one's favourite way to spend a day. However, it doesn't have to be terrible. After all, going in to the hospital voluntarily for an hour is always going to be preferable to going for a long stay out of necessity. It is also means you're less likely to be catheterised.

Result!

F

FITNESS
I Worry About You, You Know

I know I'm not your mother (if I were, you wouldn't be allowed out with that haircut), but I am still concerned about your well-being. No one is getting any younger these days, and where would I (and my book sales receipts) be if my beloved fans started dropping dead prematurely?

So we need to get you back into fighting shape.

We'll start by getting rid of your bad habits. Habits are hard to break, I know, and I shan't pretend they aren't. But come on now, you're all big boys and need to get a grip on things. If you watch more than two hours of telly a day, stop. No more trips to the chippy. And stop buying apps for your phone. Now. They say it takes three weeks to break a habit, so be patient and you'll get through.

Once your habits are gone, you're going to have a lot more time on your hands. That time should be spent doing one of the following options: taking a walk in the fresh air, doing some light stretches, cooking and eating healthier meals, ordering and then reading more of my work or spending some time in quiet solitude contemplating what your purpose here actually is. This last one may be rough going early on, but once your head is cleared of Angry Birds, greasy food and *TOWIE*, things will start falling into place, I promise.

If you keep up this routine for the next three weeks, you'll be healthier and happier. If for any reason you're not, you might want to purchase my book *Stop Listening To Others and Live Your Own Life For Once*, which recently hit the shops.

FOCUS
Baby, You Can Drive My Car

Yes, I drive. I am always offended by those who assume I do not: they are also the people who assume women of a certain age should not smoke or wear trousers. Why people continue to perpetuate such stereotypes is beyond me.

I received my first driving permit at the tender age of sixteen, as part of the traditional American rite of passage: the blow of the loss of one's virginity is softened somewhat by a license to drive. My first car was in fact not a car at all, but a pick-up truck my grandfather gave me. My grandfather was an early pioneer in alternative fuels and the truck was powered by a mixture of sawdust and corn whiskey, which, at the time, was rather difficult to find at Trenton gas stations. My grandfather was the one who taught me to drive, and he instilled in me a strong belief in three concepts of good driving: always wear a safety belt, keep your eyes on the wheel and maintain a reasonable distance behind the car in front (particularly if it's covered in bumper stickers). Because of his excellent advice, I am proud to say that I have rarely been involved in any vehicular manslaughter cases.

Sadly, it appears that many drivers today were not taught by such clever and inventive instructors. What's made it worse is the fact that there are now more and more distractions in cars; the modern driver not only has FM radio to listen to but also mobile phones, crying children and the woman on the sat-nav giving him directions to the nearest offie. Our lives are full of hustle and bustle, but this hustle and bustle must stop when one's pistons are, if you'll pardon my French, pumping. It takes a responsible driver to say, "No, I cannot focus only on the road when I have the introduction to my autobiography to proofread as well as sign these photos to get out for the afternoon post." Therefore these days, I prefer to be a passenger. Having Christopher drive allows me to use my time wisely without putting myself or any other road users in jeopardy.

For those who find themselves unable to "turn off the world" even when behind the wheel, please realise the risks you are taking. I appreciate that not everyone has the luxury of having a young, attractive man to motor her around -- for those who don't, I'm afraid public transport may be your only recourse. Don't cry about it.

Despite what Jeremy Clarkson says, dangerous driving does not make one "big" or "clever." When you next get in the car, if you can't be sure that you will ignore your phone ringing or your pager going off or your children setting each other's hair on fire, I suggest that you make alternative arrangements. The life you save may be your own or, more importantly, Cheryl Cole's. And even if you are prepared to take that chance, waiting for your lifeless corpse to be retrieved from the middle of the northbound lane of the M25 is certain to slow down traffic so try to think of others for once in your life, will you?

FRIENDSHIP
Everyone Needs An Algonquin

When I was breakfast editor for Rupert Stanley Quim's magazine *Specific Monthly*, I often found myself eating lunch at the famous (or infamous) Cafe Grandmother. It was not unusual for the likes of detective writer Derek Pinpoint, novelist Ginger Readers and her cronies and other notable writers to join me. I recall us gossiping, eating blueberry pancakes and BLT sandwiches and generally just having a smashing time. Reminiscing about these years brings to mind another group of quick wits who gathered at a round table, throwing their coins down, telling secrets, cracking jokes and sleeping with each others' mates. I am thinking, of course, of my mother's bridge group in Trenton, New Jersey.

These ladies would get together each Tuesday afternoon, most often at our house since we seemed to have, based on the women's weekly comments, the nicest drapes. In retrospect I suppose it was our ever full liquor cabinet that really drew them in, but I wouldn't want to hurt my mother's feelings. If she had them. But I remember as a youngster sitting at the top of the stairs, peering down at the lacquered hairstyles, the crossed legs and the cigarettes burning down to ash. I can hear now in my mind's eye the laughing which grew in both intensity and decibels as the day wore on (and the liquor bottles drained). I remember the voices, hushed but excited, sharing secrets and insults (the words "embezzling" and "stupid bastard," to this day, take me back to those innocent afternoons), and I so wanted to grow up to be one of those ladies. (I had hoped by the time I was old enough to lacquer my hair, another one of the ladies would have bought nicer drapes so we could meet elsewhere, thereby excluding my mother.) But unfortunately I found that, as I grew older, this sort of bonding had become a thing of the past. If I had not been blessed with such talent as a writer, I may never have even experienced those few years with Derek, Ginger and friends. The days of intimates getting together to enjoy the misery of others just simply don't exist in our work-a-day world.

Which leads me to my point that young people today just seem too isolated. My advice to them, and to you, reader, if you find yourself lonely or disconnected, is to get married. Too many young people stay single, "trying to find themselves." That's not what life is about. Life is about alcoholic laughs and betrayal and embezzlement. The burdens of a spouse lead directly to that kind of happiness. Just ask my mother or her friend, Dolores. They're both listed, but don't bother calling on a Tuesday afternoon. Or just call my parents' house then, but hang up when she answers. That really gets her goat.

Best of luck, little ones!

G

GLORY
The Weird And Wonderful -- The City Centre

I had the pleasure of escorting an American friend on a sightseeing trip today. He was traveling to Newcastle for a conference on the literary implications of nose-blowing, so I took the train up to meet him. Instead of hitting the usual tourist spots, we simply wandered around the City Centre before he nipped off to deliver his paper, *Congestion in Nabokov's Novels*. (I unfortunately was unable to stay to hear his fascinating research, but I'm sure it went down a storm).

One of the things he commented on was the exciting array of pedestrians in the City Centre. He took great pleasure in hearing apologies from the number of elderly ladies who ran over his feet with their shopping trolleys, and he was particularly impressed with the teenagers pushing their babies' prams, dodging the dedicated charity workers desperately harassing the early morning shoppers in the name of a good cause. While he was slightly less thrilled by the young lad taking the piss in front of McDonalds (I mean this, unfortunately, literally), he had to laugh at the good-natured way said lad dealt with the restaurant's manager who attempted to shoo him from the premises. He even maintained his smile as he gave his witness statement to the police.

I do love showing my American friends around English city centres. They so encapsulate the glory of the nation. They are hot beds of activity, and much of it is so very English. I myself still adore wandering through the markets; their mystery I initially approached as a novelty, but even to this day, I do my best to support as many stalls as I can. This may explain why I have a cupboard full of striped knee socks and bags of outdated, non-brand-name crisps which will never see the light of day. But I feel I've done my part to support my community by purchasing them, and that's all a citizen can do.

The other thing I love about city centres is the great pride people take in them. The pedestrian areas are clean; litter seems to immediately be snatched up by the thoughtful and conscientious beggars who then feed it to their dogs. What community spirit! While we have to face the fact that city centres often do have problems, I am so chuffed when I see locals taking an active stand about the unfortunate but sadly inevitable crimes that often take place in urban areas. I take off my fine feathered hat to the commitment these men and women make to maintaining their municipal duties.

City centres often get negative press but I, for one, find them absolutely delightful. I would happily spend a day wandering any English city centre, as long as I can get out of there before dark. I'd kill myself before I went into a city centre at night. I have civic pride, but I'm not a fucking idiot.

GRACE
Where Was His Stethoscope?

As you are all aware, I try to stay out of party politics as I feel, in doing so, I could possibly be seen as abusing my influence over the general public. In a world where young girls are encouraged to cut their hair in what ever style they see fit and boys are no longer required to wear cuff links, a sensible role model such as myself is literally a god-send. However, an incident recently occurred which has forced me to speak out on what is generally called an "issue." Please accept this apology in advance, as I know you will be both sympathetic and undoubtedly moved to action.

For a fortnight, my stomach had been giving me trouble. I spent quite some time trying to locate the source of the upset. Initially I thought that it might have been the seafood I had eaten while dining with our local MP. However, having eaten several times at this particular restaurant (Monty's, a lovely establishment, be sure to ring ahead to book the corner table), I realised that in no way could it be possible that Maurice had served us anything but the highest standard of food. The weather has been unseasonably hot so I questioned whether or not that was upsetting the aforementioned organ. This did not seem a possibility either, though, as I have been determinedly fanning myself and sitting in the breeze whenever one was available.

Eventually, my dear friend Alice Wintergarden convinced me that I should book an appointment to see a doctor. I hold up my hands to the fact that I have not attended our surgery for over nine years, due, of course, to my family's impeccably healthy heredity and reliance on whiskey as a sleeping aid. I was disappointed to hear that Mr Skirmey, my previous personal physician, had since passed away (why was this not mentioned in the local papers, I ask?) and further distraught when told that I would have to wait to see any available doctor. I considered slamming down the phone in a huff; however, the additional stress of being treated as dirt had worsened my pain, so I duly went to wait at the surgery as instructed.

Waiting rooms are always a joy, no matter what you are waiting for, because of the wide selection of unusual people who seem to occupy them. This waiting room was no different. There was a large percentage of older people, and I noticed that most of the old dears were unable to hear their names being called. I helpfully pointed this out to the receptionist and suggested a more effective tannoy system; however, her reaction could only be described as a rebuff. Additionally two young mothers came in with babies and, although I am never one to judge, their lack of wedding rings most certainly would have contributed to whatever was causing their children to be so poorly and quite frankly unattractive.

When I was finally called, I walked into a room to be greeted by a young man who introduced himself as Doctor Robert. I could not tell if Robert was his Christian name or family name, but this issue soon became moot when I realised he did not have a stethoscope around his neck. What on earth has become of our health service today when such a basic medical requirement is so flagrantly ignored? Additionally I noted (as I was already beginning my letter of complaint in my mind's eye) that he continually referred to me as Mrs Whitt-Wellington, though both my form and file clearly state that I have yet to marry. Such thoughtlessness.

But the area of most distress is still yet to come, and I warn fragile readers to look away now. My examination, if it could be called such, consisted of being told to lie on a bed clearly designed for a streetwalker and lift my blouse. I was then prodded in a way that was most disturbing, followed by Mr Robert tucking his thick fingers underneath the band of my skirt. (I should stress that this assault came without warning and, given my limited time working as a volunteer nurse in the Congo, I deduced that there seemed to be no need for him to intrude on my person in such a way).

He then told me to sit up and asked me if I had been passing wind. What kind of question is that for a young man to ask a woman of my stature and upbringing? When I refused to acknowledge his question, he then asked if I was suffering from a productive cough. This was the last straw. I could not even understand what the poor lad meant -- the only thing that I'm aware any cough could produce is an awkward glance while at the opera. I readjusted my Lillian Cranium silk floral blouse and excused myself from his office.

Has the medical world become this merry-go-round of silliness and irrelevance in the last nine years? Where is the grace that used to be essential in the practice of medicine? I think of the poor people who must attend the surgery on a more regular basis than I, perhaps for an injection of some sort. How do they bear it? I urge all of you to consider my experience and those of other victims when casting your ballot at the next election. I believe it is the only way we can return to the time when physicians were willing to prescribe any medication you had read about in your ladies' magazine. Ah, the good old days!

A final note: please, do not send flowers as you'll be grateful to know that my condition has improved immensely. After the whole sordid affair, Alice poured me a glass or two to help me compose myself and that night I was finally able to sleep the upset away.

GRATITUDE
Thank You, Driver, For Getting Me Here

If you're like me, you probably grew up admiring lion tamers. Like Superman, lion tamers' incredible talents, fantastic costumes and determination to do good for humanity are inspirational and sexually intriguing. Unfortunately, we all learn as we age that neither Superman nor lion tamers exist in the real world.

However, there are stylish, altruistic hard workers who walk among us. We see them everyday but rarely do we take a moment to either notice or appreciate them. They are bus drivers.

Hey, hey, hey now, Agatha (I hear you saying). Hay is for horses (I hear my elocution tutor saying). Please hear me out.

Often you'll see in the editorial pages of the tabloids complaints about the buses: the stink of piss, the teenagers' noise, the slight delays that on occasion may occur. These are simply hooey. Take it from a frequent rider (yes, I ride the bus, what of it?): our public transport system is champion and it is due primarily to the humble and skilful bus driver.

Every single day in England, men (and I'll admit a few women) risk their lives for our safety. Plenty of people bitch (excuse my French), but how many of you can manoeuvre that much steel and human cargo through the dangerous streets of our country without killing someone? Let's not forget that the average English street is barely wider than the average English bus. Once when I was on the Number 41 into the city, our bus driver managed to squeeze by an illegally parked Vauxhall Nova, passing the wing mirror with literally just an inch to spare. He neither blinked nor broke a sweat. That's power.

Bus drivers must maintain this cool through other stresses, very often from the passengers they devote their lives to. We might be frustrated with other riders' noise, confusion or lack of correct change, but these poor chaps have to deal with it for hours on end and they're not allowed to slap or swear at any of them. They are also our guardians while we ride: I remember so clearly the day a fight broke out in the back of the Shopper Hopper and within seconds, the driver jumped from his seat, disarmed the attacker and quickly citizen-arrested him. Not impressive enough for you? I should add that during that same trip, our driver also performed cardiopulmonary resuscitation on an old dear, led us all in a sing-song and still managed to get us to the Supercentre right on time.

There are very few heroes left in the world today, but for me, bus drivers come closest to being modern day lion tamers. I just wish more wore hats. And carried whips.

H

HANKY PANKY
You Love It And You Know It

Whether you are a devoted creationist or a sensible evolutionist, you've got to admit there's a beautiful logic behind the fact that nothing on earth is more pleasurable for human being than a little hanky panky. Not everyone's body is capable of shifting bricks, dancing in stilettos or breaking hula-hoop world records, but everyone can enjoy a good roll in the hay. This is something on which we all, from Papa Franciscus to Richard Dawkins, must surely agree.

Although you know I am normally reserved about sharing intimate information, I must confess that I have known a few lovers in my time (three just this week, actually). I make no bones about this. In fact, in many ways I feel it's my contribution to improving the global human condition. Doing my part to spread a little happiness, however temporary (though ideally around the forty-five minute mark), can only be a good thing for a world where bigotry, hatred and despair dominate the headlines. When I do it, I don't just do it for myself or even for the other person(s) involved -- I do it for all of humanity. Lesser women might see that responsibility as intimidating; I see it as an honour and a privilege.

There can be something otherworldly about sex. *La petite mort* brings us to that penultimate moment in life -- we could "cross over" into Eternity but instead we fall back on the bed and light up a fag. I can't remember which of the Romantic poets wrote that his lover "brought him closer to God," but it's a beautiful and true description of that ecstasy.

While sex can be mystical, it can also be extremely practical. Let's say you've had an absolutely distressing day at the office and are looking forward to getting home to enjoy a glass of *Château Lafite Rothschild* and a lovely meal. However, once you get home, you realise all you've got in is *Pichon Lalande* and there's no asparagus in the crisper. At this moment, relaxation is paramount. A quick unzip and you'll be as satisfied and drowsy as you would have been had you gone to dinner at the club (plus there's no need to put your tie back on). And unless you're a Premiership footballer, you will have saved yourself a few bob as well.

Whether it was a night with one of my many one true loves or my first time on Concorde or even that initially confusing but ultimately captivating afternoon at summer camp, the memories of all of my sexual experiences make me glad to be alive. I am more than grateful that human bodies, when pressed together in any of many various positions, can lead to such wonderful explosions of love, passion and a certain amount of viscous fluids.

HEALTH
It Does A Body Good

I do not mind saying that my body is far from perfect. Very few bodies are, though some come close. However, I am utterly devoted to keeping my physical form as firm and flourishing as my intellectual faculties. You know I am particular about what I eat, and my medicine cabinet is always well stocked with vitamins (choose your own pronunciation). Even when the weather is less than welcoming, I face the slight nip in the air to take my morning constitutional. Christopher has shown me his preferred workout, and although the drills are intense, I think the pink blush the exertion brings to my cheeks makes me look quite vivacious.

There are some health concerns, though, that we individuals cannot manage on our own. For those, we need to consult what are commonly known as "professionals." I use the term extremely delicately. Unfortunately, there are quite a few bunco artists polluting many of our nation's doctors' offices. For example, I cannot respect a man who suggests expectorating phlegm as a remedy, despite any number of certificates decorating his office walls. So take care, readers: I caution all of you to be sure of to whom you are trusting yourself with.

But don't go crazy. We do need those who are truly experts. Please understand that I am not encouraging anyone to perform their own dental work. I have seen this done, and it's horrifying. I know some suffer from odontophobia, but it is quite important to get one's dental groove on at least once every six months.

However, while I never hesitate to welcome a qualified man into my mouth (providing that he's gloved up, of course), I do confess to feeling just a tiny bit anxious about visiting the eye doctor. Now before you start making assumptions about age-related macular degeneration, I can testify that my nerves have nothing to do with refusing to accept that I am getting older. I am getting older, but you know what, so are you so shut up anyway. I do sometimes wear spectacles and if I were ever to be asked to wear bifocals, I'd take it like a man. I don't like going to get my eyes examined simply because of the close proximity of the doctor to my person. I am usually suspect when I feel a stranger's breath on my face (excluding that wonderful evening in Paris), so I don't know why it should be any different just because he's wearing a white tabard. Plus I always seem to get the one whose wife leaves him dissatisfied, and the room ends up being so thick with sexual tension that I've no doubt my ocular accuracy is compromised. This is why I never go to the same optometrist twice -- there's something that rubs me wrong about sharing such intimacy, being expected to pay for it and then hearing nothing from him again until I receive a brief postcard a year later, saying it'd be lovely to see me.

I bring this up only because said epistle arrived this morning. I had Christopher ring up our village's newest specialist (after instructing him to spend a few hours researching the man's background and I was quite impressed by his Facebook photo). I have also faxed over my curriculum vitae, a photo and a few notable newspaper clippings. At least this way, he and I will have some sort of relationship before he gets all up in my face next month. And this one is single as well.

We all must take advantage of both our internal and external resources to keep our bodies well. Those who don't often get quite poorly, some die and others, well, they do okay so perhaps it doesn't matter.

Actually, whatever. It's your life if you're happy pissing it away.

HOME
A Welcome Mat

There's nowt wrong with being house proud. Think about it. It's the place where you spend time with the things you love most: your partner, your children or, more likely, your telly, so why wouldn't you want it to look as lovely and comfortable as possible?

Of course, if you're rather flabby in the cash department, you can do whatever you want to your house. But everyone can and should make their home -- whether it's a million pound property in Mayfair or a cardboard box under a bridge -- beautiful and welcoming.

I'd like to share some tips that you, regardless of annual income, can use to increase pride and resale value of your home. Firstly, do something about your garden. It's not difficult to do: a few flowers and a patch of grass will do the trick. Do not, however, display anything that could be described as an "ornament." Whether your intention is to be whimsical, religious or racist, lawn ornaments are never as fascinating as you think they are. Do not let anything litter your garden. This includes children's toys, litter (obviously), discarded newspapers and pizza delivery brochures, or plastic lawn furniture. I refuse to enter houses when I see these things outside; you should, too, which will make it rather difficult for you if it's your own home we're talking about.

Inside your home, there are a few definite do's and don'ts. Don't use wallpaper. Yes, it might have once been clever, but we're living in the 21st century now, people, we all know plaster and paint go on walls. Walls do not have to be Magnolia, but do use colour carefully. If you find yourself needing to don sunglasses to avoid a migraine attack, you may have chosen unwisely. Keep it reasonable.

Houseplants are another simple and important aspect to making a house a home. They are relatively easy to care for, so are particularly wise for bachelors: they show that you acknowledge that there are other living things in the world besides yourself, yet you won't be investigated by the RSPCA when you forget to water them and ditch them in your rubbish bin.

Each room in your home should have a specific purpose and a door so that those purposes do not ever cross pollinate. The bathroom is for bathing, the sitting room is for sitting, the bedroom is for sleeping and the panic room is for panicking. If you ever find yourself feeling panicky in the bedroom, you are confusing purposes so leave immediately (or call a cab for the person bouncing around on top of you). An organised home is a happy home.

Of course, a person's home must reflect their personal tastes, so I can't be too specific with my suggestions. You have the right to fill your house with whatever crap you prefer (just as I have the right to refuse to enter if I find it too repulsive). But whatever it is, take some pride in it.

A sow holds her head high in her pigsty. Don't you deserve to feel just as satisfied amidst your own muck? I believe you do and should.

I

INCOME
Money, It's A Gas

I've never had time for people who badmouth money, especially when those people are rolling in it. "Money is the root of all evil": really, Reverend? So why are you driving that Cadillac? "Money can't buy you love": money might not have bought Lennon and McCartney love (though I bet it did), but it did buy them lots and lots of really, really nice shit.

I won't patronize you by saying that money's more trouble than it's worth or that life without it is just as fine. The truth is money is great. I should know, I have tons of it and I live a very rich life.

Let me tell you just a little of the role money plays in my life. Sometimes when I wake up, I fancy something -- it might be a certain kind of pastry for breakfast or some expensive tea. It might be a bouquet of out of season flowers that would simply brighten up my sitting room. One of my fingers might look a little lonely without a ring. It might even be that I have a hankering for the mist that hits one's face as she overlooks Niagara Falls. Guess what? All of those things are at my disposal, thanks to my seemingly unending supply of money.

I point this out to you not to brag (those who truly deserve the money they have are never boastful), but simply to admit what appears to be the dirtiest secret going: that it's good to have money. If you don't have any, you really ought to give it a try. Seriously, you'd be surprised how much easier, fun and jewel-encrusted it makes your life.

I do feel I need to clarify that when I speak about money, I am speaking about cold hard cash. I do not believe in using credit; I'm no financial wizard, but surely there's bound to be consequences to people buying things with money that doesn't really exist -- I can't see banks allowing that. However, the real reason behind my preference is that there's nothing like the feel of cash in one's fist. Whether I'm chucking some silver at a beggar or slipping a C-note into the panty of a stripper, the subtle friction when money slides out of my hand is a real sensual pleasure. I particularly like British Sterling as the coinage has a real weight to it, and I adore the marriage of gold and silver on the two pound coins. Every time I get one of them, I put it into my special money box, which Christopher has used on three occasions to knock senseless an intruder in the house (milkmen should never come in uninvited, even if the door is on the latch).

Sid James once said, "If you got it, spend it. If you ain't got it, get it." I really don't know why more people don't take this advice to heart. I spend my money like it's going out of style. I realise I am fortunate that my piggy bank allows me to do this, but even those will smaller digits in their balance columns should be willing to blow some dough from time to time. Spending is a way to contribute towards strengthening the economy, which strengthens our country, which strengthens the global community. If that's not a good enough reason to love money, I don't know what is. Except maybe all the stuff it gets you -- stuff is a pretty good reason as well.

INTERACTION
Woo And How To Pitch It

Men. You gotta love them, what with their briefcases, insecurities, external genitalia and all.

Recently one of my admirers enquired about the ideal way to woo a lady of my cachet. I was charmed by his moxie as well as his attached photo, so I immediately began a detailed response to his query. However, I realised that he may not be the only young man feeling a bit overwhelmed by the changes in the "dating game," so I've decided to take this opportunity to share my advice with all of you losers.

- Ignore any advice given to you by another man (father, brother, that man your mother asked you to call uncle even though he's really just her "special friend"). They don't know what they're talking about. If they did, they'd be too busy shagging to have time to stick their noses into your love life.

- Better yourself before you even think about getting involved with a woman. Seriously, look at yourself -- who in their right mind would be interested in knobbing that? Read a few books, learn a foreign language, watch a few films. Before you put yourself "on the market," you've got have a product others would be interested in purchasing or at least renting with the option to buy.

- In addition to building up your mind, keep your body in reasonable shape. While not all women demand perfection in the male physique, we do have some standards. Update your wardrobe -- remember, you are what you wear. Hygiene is also important. I mean, do I really have to be telling you these things? No wonder you're alone.

- Be bold when approaching a woman you're interested in. Don't be afraid to go up to a woman you don't know and introduce yourself. Yes, you may get pepper sprayed a few times. But surely you can cope with having profound vision loss in one eye if it means finding Miss Right.

- When talking to a woman, limit the amount of references to your penis to zero. Men are fascinated by cock talk but women, less so, so keep it confined to the locker room. Extremely unattractive is discussing others' opinions of your member. Women aren't particularly interested in the testimony of others, whether it's from previous users or doctors who specialise in abnormalities.

- It's true that to curry a woman's favour, a man should steer the talk towards the lady herself. This isn't because women are the vainer sex; it's because they are the more interesting sex. Do you know how boring it is to hear a man talk about himself? Ask your mental health counsellor or parish priest, they'll tell you.

- Ask her questions, as long as you're prepared to accept the answers. If you're not going to be able to handle the fact that she is better than you at almost everything, you may struggle.

- If things are going swimmingly, it's perfectly acceptable to try your chances on the first date. Gently touch her hand or knee, give her a quick peck on the cheek. If she doesn't press charges, you're in there, my son.

- If things are going less than swimmingly, wrap up the interaction quickly. You're not doing anyone any good by prolonging the inevitable awkwardness. Don't worry that she might have her feelings hurt. If you haven't enjoyed the date, it's unlikely she's found much to write home about either. Cut your losses, make your apologies and vacate the premises, leaving as few contact details and as little DNA as possible.

Following the above advice should help you make a start towards finding love. It's not an easy task, but my motto has always been the harder, the better. When it comes to love, the challenge of finding it is always worth the pay off of receiving it.

INTIMIDATION
Are You Being Bullied?

It's school time again, and students of all ages are sharpening their pencils, pressing their uniforms and buffing up their saddle shoes (yes, I'm talking about masturbation). Sadly, in addition to homework stress and test anxiety, school can also give rise to bullying. The legal definition of bullying is:

> *1. Getting all up in someone else's face for no good reason, 2. Being cruel to someone simply because they are different (usually better) than you, 3. Just acting like a real dick*

Of course, bullying doesn't just happen to children; grown ups can be victims as well, especially if they're great big babies about everything.

If you feel like you are being bullied, here are a few proactive steps you can take:

1. Hold your hand up to the bully's face and state in a firm but calm voice, "Bullying is wrong. Stop bullying me, you big bully." Give the bully the worst stink eye you can muster. This should help the bully see what a total bell-end he (or she, let's be fair here) is being. This is particularly effective if you can do it in unison with other people, to show everyone that bullying will not be silently tolerated.

2. Report the bullying to a person in power -- a form tutor, principal, boss or head of the FBI. Keep clear documentation to present as evidence. If you've filmed the bullying, you should <u>not</u> post it to online, even though I bet it'd inspire some hilarious comments.

3. There is strength in numbers, so offer other victims support. Start an anti-bullying support group. But don't call it that. Refer to it as "Football Club" or "Art Group." Don't ask for trouble.

I do not advocate attacking the bully -- avoid violent actions or violent words. Fighting back like this is never a good idea: firstly, it takes you down to the bully's level; secondly, look at your scrawny body. That bully is going to kick the shit out of you, and how's that going to help anyone?

Of course, it can be beneficial to remember that bullies bully because they are actually sad, insecure or damaged. If that knowledge gives you some pleasure, make the most of it. Also, you might find it helpful to know that studies show that 99.157% (probably) of bullies end up living miserable lives, either in prison, mental institutions or cabinet positions. They'll suffer eventually, don't you worry.

If by chance, you are the bully -- all I can say is shame on you. I've no respect for bullies, and I strongly encourage you to change your ways, dickhead.

J

JEOPARDY
Health And Safety Be Damned

As Lou Reed proved with multiple examples (Holly, Candy, Little Joe), a walk on the wild side can be beneficial.

(If you think I'm talking about going into the City Centre after eleven, let me assure you <u>I am not</u>. That's just stupid.)

Instead I am referring to sometimes choosing the tough option, pushing the boat out a bit, going for the gusto, mixing cocaine with heroin -- taking a few chances for once in your life.

Looking back into my own past, some of my greatest achievements have been the result of my willingness to shake things up a bit, refusing to always play it safe. For example, the very first piece of writing I ever submitted for publication, I did so at a great risk to my physical person. I had been struggling with horrible writer's block, but luckily I had a stroke of brilliance the very day of the deadline. However, to get the submission into the post on time, I was forced to skip my *bojuka* class, which meant that, if I ever were confronted by a violent street assault (which luckily I have not been), I would not be at the "top of my game."

Now it's not always necessary to take it to such an extreme. It might be as simple as using quarters instead of nickels at your weekly poker game, telling your boss to fuck off or agreeing to be set up on a blind date. Sometimes we allow ourselves to get too comfortable, and we don't move forward. Think about this: undoubtedly someone on your street decided to improve their property's value by putting in a pond, quickly realised that it would require upkeep and figured why bother. The poor koi went belly up; even the toads abandoned it after that stray cat drowned and began the process of decomposition. That pond is stagnant. Never taking a risk means your life is stagnant. Is that what you want? Dead fish and cats?

Taking a few chances with your life can spice it up a bit. But just watch out for double jeopardy -- that's illegal, don't forget.

JUDGMENT
Judge Not Lest Ye Cast The First Stone Into Your Own Glass House

I, like many of you, spent the weekend reading and listening to reports about the latest headline-grabbing scandal.

Unlike many of you, I am very familiar with the key player, Bartholomew Peetlemen. Of course, when I say very familiar, I mean I know him, I've had dinner with him, have been to have his home. I am familiar with him, but not in the coochie-coochie way, if that's what you're driving at.

Barth, or as the papers have dubbed him "Mr Peetlemen," seems to have got himself embroiled in what is becoming a typical disgrace of the financially secure: tax evasion through his accountant who runs a money-making scheme with an unnamed footballer. Plus it turns out the accountant is a prostitute who got a gastic band on the NHS and has been selling blood for oil to Kony (2012).

I shan't be defending him here: I always found him very likeable, but he is, of course, just a man, with the vulnerabilities and failings (premature ejaculation) of any other man. Whether he got involved due to selfish greed or stupid ignorance, he must now face the consequences of the decisions he's made.

Everyday on the news we see people whom we previously viewed as monuments of success and dedication crumble into piles of shameful, useless pebbles and dust. Many respond with angry exclamations of "Give 'em what he deserves" while others surrender to a sort of *que sera, sera* attitude.

I try not to judge the mighty when they fall, because I'm concerned that these issues are indicative of a larger problem -- something inherently wrong with our society, perhaps our very souls. What this fault is I have yet to determine, but you'll be the first to know when I get it figured out.

JUSTICE
The Last Piece Of Cake

Punishment: it isn't all bad. We look at countries where those who steal have their hands cut off, where those who betray are thrown out of the community, where those who murder are murdered themselves. Certainly, those of us living in a civilized world would never approve of such measures. Though our punishments may be different, they serve the same purpose: a wrongdoer must get her comeuppance. Our society would fail to function if we could not be assured of this belief.

I first witnessed this precept beautifully illustrated many years ago. I will never forget the date: it was sometime in April when I was anywhere between seven and fourteen years old. My mother and two of her bridge-playing girlfriends had insisted that I come with them to see a young artist who was giving a talk at the State Museum. My mother had won the tickets through a radio contest (I believe she had correctly guessed the weight of the DJ's recently shaved beard clippings). I was dragged along to make up the foursome (my father had refused to go as he believed it was bad luck to be the only man walking with a trio of women).

I have always loved the State Museum; even as a child, I could see myself in so many of the breathtaking exhibits on display there. However, I had not been keen to attend the event, only because it meant spending an afternoon with Shakespeare's Weird Sisters. On the way into the building, I caught my reflection in the window glass -- I was wearing a particularly nice hat -- and decided to just keep as much distance between them and myself and try to enjoy the afternoon.

The gallery was quite packed (luckily, there were only eight other radio prize winners there and, believe you me, they were easily recognisable). My mother and her friends sat in the front row (so obvious), but I chose a seat closer to the back, where the lighting more subtly accented my striking features. The artist, she went only by the name Melinda, was beautiful. I can see her now in my mind's eye as clear as if I had seen her yesterday. She had long blonde hair, gorgeously tanned shoulders, penetrating eyes and shades of midnight blue paint staining her fingertips. I was transfixed by her and hung on every word of her speech on whatever it was she was talking about. When she finished, I gave her a standing ovation. As people began milling out, I was horrified to see that my mother and her cronies had cornered Melinda. Although I had hoped to speak to her myself, I could not think of anything worse than being identified with those three, so I did my best to sneak out of the room unnoticed. I escaped to the bathroom, where I splashed some water to cool my reddened cheeks.

However, the humiliation was far from over. I was galled to hear that my mother had arranged for Melinda to come over to our house later that evening. This meant that the next few hours were spent in a rushed panic, my mother desperate to stage a scene which implied she was a more interesting woman than she was. She stopped at the most expensive florist and bakery in town. Once we got home, I hoped my father would put his foot down, but, as usual, she disregarded him completely. In fact, she forced my father to shave (despite the fact that it was a Saturday) before Melinda's arrival, as she had the nerve to claim "we artists find stubble repellent." She put me in charge of hoovering (her not giving me the responsibility of arranging the flowers indicates her level of ignorance). By eight o'clock, we were ready to greet Melinda.

My, how the time flew by! Melinda entertained us with incredible stories of her adventures across the country, doing everything a bohemian artist should be doing. I was enthralled and felt I was getting a glimpse into my own future. Luckily, Melinda's fascinating chestnuts -- peppered with details of colours, sounds, and smells -- kept my mother silent for the majority of the night. This fact alone, I think, helped charm my father, who was quickly as seduced as I.

Around midnight, Melinda was clearly tiring. She had explained when she first arrived that she was flying out the following morning to show some work in an offbeat gallery in Trois-Rivières. However, my mother, it seemed, was not ready to bid the artist farewell. She dragged out some of her own paintings and asked Melinda for some constructive criticism. It was torturous.

In an effort to wrap things up, my father began tidying up the dishes. My mother admonished him for "rushing our guest" when there was still a piece of cake left. The room went silent. I wondered whether my father would take his usual, easy route of surrendering to my mother's vicious tongue or if Melinda's presence had changed his life in the way I already knew she had changed mine.

However, before he had a chance to decide what to do, Melinda stood up. "It's a wonderful thing to have such a conscientious husband," she said to my mother. "He's right, though, it is time for me to go." She stepped over my mother's canvases to make her way to collect her coat.

"But Melinda," my mother cried, "Please eat the last piece of cake." My father sat back down. I was frozen in the tension of the moment.

"No, Mrs Whitt-Wellington, I will not eat the last piece of cake."

Melinda came over and gave me a peck on the cheek. She walked over to my father and extended her hand. I silently prayed that he would grab her, wrap his arms around her slender figure and the three of us would walk out of my mother's house forever. But he didn't. He shook her hand. Melinda passed my mother on her way to the door, gently touching her shoulder. And then she was gone.

Seeing my mother taken down a peg for once in her bloody life has stayed with me all these years. I shall never forget that moment (probably because I replay it in my mind at least twice a day). She did wrong, and wrongdoers must eventually reap what they sow. I am so grateful that I was there to witness it.

Justice served.

K

KARMA
One Day You'll Pay, You'll All Pay

I am not one to hold grudges.

Many of you have wronged me in the past (yes, I'm talking about you), but while I don't forget (I can't help it, I've just got an excellent capacity for memory), I do forgive. That's just the kind of person I am. I'm lovely like that.

But I am a strong believer in karma. I've always felt a strong connection to the religions of the East. The months I spent studying in the Kodaikanal Mountains were so enlightening. I have tried to embrace the lessons I learned there (though, unlike some, I haven't turned them into marketing tools). Many Indian spiritual traditions believe in karma, the idea that we reap the fruits of our actions, good or bad. Even many Christians hold a similar view, so I've got a whole bucket load of gods backing me up on this theory.

I bring this up only because my wonderfully thoughtful mother has pimped me out yet again as official travel guide to the sights and sounds of England. For the past four days, I have had to have Christopher ferry around the Harringtons, my auntie and uncle twice removed. This is their first trip abroad, perhaps their first trip out of New Jersey for all I know, and my mother promised them I would keep them entertained.

I did not win "Hostess of the Year" eleven consecutive times for nothing, so it's not that I am reluctant to help relatives enjoy their holiday. It's just that these particular people are not among my favourites. It all goes back to my tenth birthday. In addition to reaching double digits, I had recently won both the county science fair (for my informative and graphically detailed project on human reproduction) as well as the Brownstone Book Prize for my second novel, *A Mother of No Importance*. Needless to say, I was the belle of the ball at Chuck E Cheese's that day. The

Harringtons didn't normally come to our family celebrations; however, this particular weekend they apparently had had a coupon for a free drink with a large pepperoni so decided to grace us with their presence. I should note that they arrived without a gift, a deliberately hostile act so they would stand out amidst all the other well-wishers. They spent most of the time feeding their faces but when they did approach my table, the only thing they could say was "Agatha, you'd best grow out that hair or you are never going to catch yourself a man."

Even at that tender age, I realised what a horrid thing that was to say to a young girl, so I blanked them and dove into the balls to join my true friends. The Harringtons were never welcome in our home again (to clarify, my mother did have them over, but each time I refused to welcome them).

As a believer in karma, I knew that this act of cruelty was bound to come back to harm them one day. As it turns out, today was the day. While they were out shopping, my aunt found a Piazza Sempione Lamb Leather Jacket she was just dying to have, but the shop did not accept travellers' cheques, and my uncle had no other way to fund the purchase. They returned home, embarrassed and empty-handed.

All I'm saying is what goes around comes around. It may have taken many years, but the negative energy they sent out that day in Trenton, New Jersey has now returned to them sevenfold.

I take no real pleasure in this fact, save for knowing that all is right in the world once more.

KICKS
If You Have Hair, Let It Down On Occasion

It's a family tradition in the Whitt-Wellington clan to be the life of the party. It originated with my grandmother's second cousin, Daisy "Legs" Lewis, who was an original Goodtime Girl in Trenton's first vaudeville show (prop. Dominic Suspenders). Ever since then, my ancestors -- particularly the female of the species -- have had themselves some fun.

Getting your kicks is essential to feeling fulfilled in life. I don't doubt that some scientist at some university somewhere proved somehow that having fun is beneficial to the nervous system or clears up spots or something, but I've never been persuaded by mere scholarly evidence; I've seen this proven before my very eyes. Having fun keeps you fit and frolicsome.

Now "fun" is an extremely vague word: what's fun to one person isn't necessarily a ball of laughs for another. That's why it's important for each of us to invest a little time investigating what "rocks our boats." You may read of my adventures and think, "I wish I could live her life, it looks like great fun," and you, of course, would be right. But don't go chasing after someone else's good time. Never deny the things that you enjoy, whatever they be, even if they're activities that someone with even the slightest bit of class would find as tiresome as all get out.

One night when you're just teetering on the thin line between pleasantly intoxicated and bleeding bladdered, reflect on the times when you most enjoyed yourself. Write them down in a list (write legibly) and keep this paper in a safe place (I suggest pressing it between two pages in a dictionary). Once you've sobered up, resolve to do one item on the list at least once a fortnight. I can guarantee you that -- whether you're playing backgammon, going to the pictures or attending a key party-- you will feel as good as I look.

KISMET
Sometimes Fate Drops It In Our Laps

Many have queried how Christopher and I met, how two kindred souls from different generations and backgrounds were able to find each other in this great big world of bastards. Like all good romances, our story is one of fate.

One summer I had an old chum visiting me. He had recently parted company with his young friend and was feeling a bit out of sorts. I had encouraged him to come spend some time with me as I know that when I'm feeling down, nothing cheers me more than being in the presence of someone of great intellect and sex appeal.

However, despite a few days' worth of my entertaining him with my usual array of amusing anecdotes and revealing dresses, he was still feeling kind of whack. I decided that surely what he needed was a new love, if not for the rest of his life at least for the remainder of the visit, as, in all honesty, his constant whinging was getting on my tits something proper. I nipped into the local working men's club for some advice on where he might find what he was looking for, and they were more than helpful. My friend and I took a taxi into the city and, following the directions that had been scribbled down for me, found our way to the club.

Now my friend is quite a good looking fellow for someone with that level of facial deformity, and it wasn't long until the young men were hanging on his every word like white on rice. We moved the group to a large table in the corner, where my friend kept the champagne flowing and the boys worked hard at keeping his pecker up. As the night wore on, I could tell that my friend was slowly whittling down his options and as the lights flashed to mark the club's closing, he had made his choice. The young man, however, was reluctant to accompany us back to my house because he had come out with someone else and did not want to leave him on his own. As he motioned towards his friend at the bar, I saw him. It was Christopher. Time seemed to stop when our eyes met. (In retrospect, the emotion of the moment was probably somewhat influenced by the ecstasy I had dropped on a dare from one of the lads.) Nonetheless, I could tell immediately that this man was going to play an important part in my life, so we invited him to join us.

He and I squeezed in next to the driver (in the backseat, trousers had already been unbuttoned, and we felt it was only right to give them as much privacy as possible). I was instantly charmed by the way Christopher shyly introduced himself as well as his willingness to tolerate my wandering hands. He explained that he normally didn't frequent such establishments but had come into the city on a similar mission to my own. The fact that both he and I were willing to go to such extremes to help our friends was a sign. Once we got back to my place, Christopher offered to make drinks while I nipped upstairs to freshen up and put some rubberized stain-resistant sheets on my guest's bed. As I tidied the rest of the room, Christopher suddenly appeared in the doorway, the light from the hallway silhouetting the manliness of his form. He asked whether he might be of some use to me around the house, and I looked him square in the trousers and accepted. (The manner in which his position was secured has since become a point of friendly debate between the two of us -- he insists he was only trying to be helpful, but when a man offers up himself to "keep me tidy," I know what he really means.) Either way, I could not refuse.

We have been inseparable ever since. Sadly, the same cannot be said for our two friends, each of whom requested that the incident never be mentioned again (a request I swore to honour until my death). Although I am not normally a believer in such things, our meeting was clearly destined. It had to have been fate that both of us had lonely and horny friends, that we both chose that particular drinking hole, that we both -- although unaware of it at the time -- were missing something in our lives that we could only find in each other. Obviously we all should be proactive in our quest for getting our needs met, but sometimes these things are out of mere mortals' control. What kismet has joined together let no man put asunder.

L

LEGACY
Last Bear In Marienbad -- A Post-Interview Addendum

I had a delightful Sunday morning being interviewed by a young journalist (he was wearing a jumper with a tie so I assume he must write for the *Guardian*). He listened graciously, took very neat notes and seemed to hit it off with Christopher, who kept him entertained when I had to interrupt the proceedings to take a phone call. The gentleman is doing research for a biography he has been commissioned to write about a dear old friend of mine, Baron Von Schwarzen Wurst, the "film" producer. Little Bear, as we used to call him, was perhaps my first real English friend (though the journalist informs me he was actually from the Duchy of Grand Fenwick, which was complete news to me). He certainly seemed English -- what with the way he was always drinking tea and backstabbing our mutual friends. In fact, in many ways, it was Little Bear who drew me across the Atlantic permanently, and I am pleased as punch his life will soon be documented so thoughtfully by my new young reporter friend.

I am obliged to keep any anecdotes about him short now as I certainly don't want to pre-empt this young man's literary masterpiece. However, soon after he left this morning, I did recall one story which brought a smile to my face, and I thought I'd share that with you all now. Bear and I had been corresponding for some time; initially an agent friend of mine had sent my photo to him as he felt I was particularly muse-like and Bear had been struggling somewhat creatively. For many months, he and I wrote long epistles about ourselves and our ideas on life, and I found him a formidable friend. (I really do rue the death of the posted letter. While email is quick and snazzy and all, it really has denied the younger generation the thrill of hearing the sound of the postman's feet on one's step and the triumph of receiving a letter that had once been in someone's hands half the way around the world and is now resting in your own.) Anyway, I was younger then and was quite well known for being "up for anything," so Bear asked me to come to London where his second "film" was soon to premiere. (His first, *Death Wore a Strapless Gown*, had been awarded a silver dong at the Pyongyang Film Festival.) That I had never actually met the man was of no concern to me; in fact, I suppose that was part of the thrill (all my life I've seemed to prefer men I've never actually met.) The trip was a whirlwind, the details of which I'm sure you'll be able to read in the forthcoming biography. However, I feel this incident, to me, really sums up the Von Schwarzen Wurst mystique.

The "film" featured a terrible actress called Mona Midnight. This was her real name, which I think gives you some indication of the faith her parents had in her intellectual ability. Mona fancied herself a bit of a stunner and, although Little Bear did sleep with her (these sort of things were contractual obligations in those days), he didn't really much care for her. The night of the premiere the cast and crew and I celebrated at Claude's, a lovely establishment where all the beautiful people used to gather (I believe it's since closed and has been replaced by a Wimpy Bar). Mona had been partaking in a few beverages and was enjoying the attention a little too much. After tolerating her behaviour for as long as he could, Bear stood up from the table, calmly announced that Mona would never be a star and dropped his cigarette into her champagne flute. He then grabbed my arm and we rushed back to the hotel, where we made love three times in quick succession after which he fell into a deep sleep that lasted for almost a week (I flew back to America on the fifth day). When Bear had regained consciousness, he sent a telegram, asking where he had left his bow tie. The moment I read that cable I knew that England was where I belonged and began making arrangements for my emigration.

Bear was a man's man and a woman's man (in other words, he went both ways). He stood for all that was right with the world and had the guts to stand up to all that was wrong with the world. His "films" should be seen by everyone. They are his legacy, and I shall never regret the time I wasted on him.

LOGIC
How To Solve A Murder

I certainly don't want to be an alarmist, but if there's one thing I've learned from crime shows on television, it's that most murders are not solved until there's at least enough mystery and intrigue to pad out a forty-two minute broadcast. I've also learned that we are all likely to be involved in crime, especially if we live in "a town where things like this just don't happen." Assuming you don't end up a murder victim (if you do, please disregard this advice), you're likely to find yourself embroiled in a crime investigation at some point, so here are some hints for wrapping it up neatly.

Gathering Evidence
1. Don't let small town cops run the show. They will walk all over evidence, forget to take photographs and allow onlookers to run amok. Get the Feds in straight away.
2. If the murder weapon is not found near the scene, check the bottom of a nearby body of water. It'll be there. It always is.
3. Any obvious clues are pointing you towards the wrong person.
4. Swab everything. Spray Luminol everywhere. Save some air from the scene in a jar; by the time this case goes cold and then is reopened years from now, they'll probably be able to get DNA from air so think ahead.

Zeroing In On A Suspect
1. The closest person to the victim is usually your best suspect. Unless the killer was a stranger. Or it might be someone the victim knew long ago or casually bumped into on the street. Interview all of these options.
2. Do surveillance. Surveillance is cool. Locations to watch are the crime scene, a nearby body of water and the killer's workplace.
3. Do not bother running the first ten suspects' DNA or fingerprints through any databases. They won't turn up any matches.
4. The last person to have seen the victim alive is the killer.

Questioning The Suspect

1. If the suspect knew the victim well, they should be hysterical 24-7. If they're not, they're the killer.

2. Check the suspect's arms for scratches. Innocent people never have scratches on their arms; it's as simple as that.

3. If the suspect sticks to the same story, it's been rehearsed. Arrest them. If their story changes at all, they're covering their tracks. Arrest them.

4. If you're filming the interrogation, be sure the camera gets your good side.

Trying The Case

1. Don't worry if you don't have a motive, weapon or any physical evidence. Those matter much less that you expect.

2. Hire a lawyer who shouts. This impresses juries, because they are easily seduced by loud noises.

3. Give due respect to the court stenographer. Too few do.

4. Get a cable news pundit on board. You're sorted.

LOVE
Are You In The Mood For It?

My good work for the community began when I was still just a slip of a girl. Despite my mother's obvious interest in no one but herself, she and my father made it clear that caring for others was essential to living a meaningful life. When I was in elementary school, I was active in a local chapter of the group Retards Are People, Too (it was a different time, you remember) until I got involved in school government where I could serve others in a more official capacity. By the time I got to high school, I had numerous volunteer roles on my resume so when I applied to be a candy striper, the hospital had no qualms about bringing me in immediately. I'll never forget the first time I got dressed for the job: luckily, my bosom had recently blossomed and to say I looked fetching would have been an understatement. (I'm proud to say I kept the outfit and when I occasionally put it on -- usually as a treat for Christopher on his birthday -- I still look as delectable as I did back then).

My first day on the job I was assigned to the old people's ward. My task was to offer them magazines, drinks of water and general good cheer. The first few I interacted with were on the grumpy side, but I did my best. The fourth bed, though, contained a woman whose story would teach me an important lesson: what you don't know can still hurt you.

Her name was Delilah, and she had only been in the hospital for a few days. She wasn't a New Jersey native but had been in town visiting an old friend when she fell ill. She had been born and raised in Chicago; in fact, this trip was the first time she had ever been this far from the Windy City. She wasn't interested in any magazines but asked if I would sit and chat with her awhile. By then I was well aware of my talents as a conversationalist, so I thought that a talk might benefit her recovery. I also welcomed a sit-down as I was unused to wearing wedge heels.

Surprisingly, Delilah seemed more interested in talking than listening, a trait I generally despise in others but in the end, I was grateful for the tale she told about falling in love for the first -- and last -- time.

She had met him at a small diner, where she sometimes worked as a waitress. His frequent stops in for what he told her was "the best Joe in town" led to innocent chats and tender flirtations. The man told her to call him Goosey, which she found appropriate since he never failed to pinch her bottom at least once during each visit. She described him as quiet but friendly -- there was something in his eyes that revealed his loving nature. But they were both shy, and their talks over coffee stayed relatively superficial. Finally, on February 13, 1929, Goosey made his move and invited Delilah to a Valentine's dance. Given the traditions of the times, he would pick her up at her family home to meet her parents before they went out for their date.

Delilah rushed home from work that day, excited to share her news with her mother. The two of them spent the evening choosing her outfit and deciding how Delilah would wear her hair. She told her mother, as she told me that day in the hospital, that there was no doubt in her mind that this was the man she was destined to marry.

That evening, Delilah, dressed to the nines, sat at the front room window, waiting for her beau to arrive. But he never did. At first she was afraid -- had something untoward happened to him? After all, Chicago was a dangerous town. But she soon realised that she had been taken for a fool: he had told her nothing about his life, she didn't even know his real name. For all she knew, he was already married and viewed their interactions as meaningless. Humiliated in front of her mother and father, she retired to her bedroom. Although she obviously eventually emerged and went on to lead a normal life, she never ever loved again.

Our conversation ended, Delilah admitted that the trip down

memory lane had tired her. But before I moved on, she grasped my hand and said, "Agatha, love is powerful. When I had it, I was never happier. When I lost it, it might as well have destroyed me." She closed her eyes and fell to sleep. When I went in for my next shift, her bed was empty.

M

MANNERS
Why The MacPhersons Are No Longer Welcome In My Home

I have always considered myself to be reasonable. Despite my wit, intelligence and influence, I eat my peas and carrots, if you know what I mean. This is why I'm terribly distraught about having to relay this story to you.

The MacPhersons do not live in my street, although they have lived "abroad," as she tells it. As is usual each January, I had an open house to let my friends catch up on all the exciting things that have happened to me during the previous year. The MacPhersons were invited by my dear friend Alice Wintergarden. I do love Alice with all my heart, but inviting people, especially the MacPhersons, to someone else's party is frowned upon where I come from (Trenton, New Jersey). Nonetheless when I greeted Alice and her chums at the door, I was more than accommodating.

Mr MacPherson (Gerald) is a rather large man. One of his eyes looks slightly to the left at all times. His wife, Elizabeth Louise, who always stands to his right, is spritely. Again, I don't mind this.

After everyone had poured themselves Harvey Wallbangers (I personally hate the taste but just adore the name!), I sat them all around me to begin my stories. I don't flatter myself a good storyteller, but the sheer magnificence of my year was bound to have them enraptured. I launched into the story about my being arrested for solicitation while accompanying a gentleman friend in Madagascar. The circumstances were quite hilarious, you may have read the account of this in the papers, and since no one was hurt (I paid a small fee and was told to button up my shirt), I knew that gales of laughter were soon to come.

But before I could stand up to imitate the bizarre walk of the police officer (he had one leg, how do these countries manage to survive in modern times?), Gerald MacPherson slumped down off his chair and on to the floor. Naturally everyone turned towards him. His wife, her own eyes going back in her head, crumpled over as well. As you know, I am a terrific hostess, so, of course, I stopped my story to see what was wrong. Once it was established that their hearts were still beating, I felt it a bit rude for them to continue to call attention to themselves in this way. (Additionally, Mrs MacPherson's skirt had risen a bit up her legs and one could see the top of her stocking.)

As I began speaking, Alice shot me a look that can only be described as acrimonious. So again I voluntarily stopped my speaking and suggested splashes of water as a way to revive the couple. Of course, these did indeed wake them up. Thankfully, they excused themselves from the festivities, and the whole ugly scene was behind us. The party went off without a hitch after that, and all of my friends left with their eyes aglaze with the wonder that is my livelihood.

However, before I could chalk this up as another successful gathering, Alice telephoned me to say that apparently the MacPhersons had had a bad reaction to the potato salad I had served. I found this not to be believed; however, I asked Alice to offer them my apologies. I graciously kept silent about the fact that it was Alice's recipe I had followed.

Having lived some time in the Orient, I am well aware of the importance of consistency with regards to guest lists, so when I began inviting people over for my "spring roundup," as it's been nicknamed by the local news media, I generously included the MacPhersons. It was Alice who responded for them: they were on holiday and expressed regret that they could not attend. I kept a brave face, but this made me realize the sad state of the world today. When moving in social circles, it is of utmost importance to have manners. This just simply cannot be overlooked despite modern day video games and dress shop prices.

Although I have never had children, I do wish that others would have taught this valuable lesson to their own offspring. So many dreadful events, such as the one above, could be avoided ,and we could all go back to the business of tee times, money laundering and family-oriented programming.

MIRACLES
In Praise Of The Wireless

There is little that brings me a sense of the almighty more so than the utter loveliness of the wireless.

Admit it, you (like I) are still a bit amazed by it. After all, we can hear another person's voice in our ears, and we do not even need a wire to do so. It is literally wireless, and that's a fact that I'm afraid most of us including our recently elected politicians often fail to remember.

Another gem the radio offers us is the repetition of up-to-date updates of current events. Say, at quarter past two, you need to nip up to the attic to retrieve an old letter written to you by one Mr Noel Coward because a so-called friend refused to believe it exists, and you miss the news bulletin. The voice on the wireless will thoughtfully repeat it for you again at two thirty. And again at two forty five. And with little change on the hour. I personally find the incessant restatement of the news reassuring: I like knowing that the only bad things happening the world have happened to someone other than me. I like being reminded of this fact every fifteen minutes even more.

While I do acknowledge that "to each his own," I must confess that I prefer to listen only to the BBC on the radio. As you know I shy away from politics, but I cannot abide a certain someone's insistence that choice is what our country needs. The BBC is what this country needs, not choice. Goodness me.

I feel enormously proud that the BBC allows women's voices to be heard on its stations, most of which I believe belong to actual women. Additionally, I find the wide range of accents and dialects incredibly refreshing. There is nothing more heart lifting than hearing that the ridiculous way that some people speak. Finally, I cannot tell you how many times Forties Cromarty

Forth Tyne Dogger has been the answer on a quiz I've been competing in (twice) so thank you, Shipping Forecast, for helping me to maintain my winning streak.

My only beef with the wireless is its attempts to place humour in the most inappropriate of places. I do not wish to hear a man sneeze while I am eating my toast in the breakfast room. I know young people find this silliness amusing, but young people also find drinking straight from a bottle legitimate, so I believe I've proved my point.

When you are next feeling down, do yourself a grand favour by turning on the wireless and letting its soothing tones take away your troubles. I see the radio as a warm bath: it washes away our cares, purifies our heads and does so without puckering our toes. You can't ask for much more than that.

And all without wires!

MYSTERY
An Encounter Between Intimates

Many years ago, I was out shopping in a rather upscale store (I don't want to give them any PR unless they are prepared to reimburse me for my trouble), when I was approached by a woman wearing incredibly large, round, black sunglasses, who asked me for the time. Now you know that I am of the belief that these items were meant to be worn out of doors (hence, the inclusion of the word "sun" in their name), but I was feeling generous and told her it was ten to eleven. She thanked me politely, and I headed over to the lingerie department, where I was known to frequently linger.

After a short time browsing, I glanced up and, through the brassieres, I saw the same woman. In any other circumstance, this would hardly be noticeable. However, this woman -- she was staring a hole right through me. I don't go looking for conflict, but I'm not afraid to meet it head on.

"Have you got some kind of problem?" I asked, moving my pocketbook to my left hand in case I needed to quickly pull the shiv from my garter.

"I was just wondering if I could ask you something," she replied.

Keeping in mind I had already provided one answer (free of charge), I was not eager to continue to engage with her. However, my intrinsic good nature meant I had to oblige.

"You've got two minutes," I said.

She pulled a notebook from her bag and approached me. She looked through, coming to a page that had a photograph taped to it.

"Do you know this man?" she asked.

Now even at that age, I was well aware that that question is always a loaded one, so I took a quick peek and said no.

"Look again," she insisted, pulling it off the page and holding it up to my face.

I took it from her. The man's face was not what I call classically handsome, but he wasn't as ugly as some I've slept with. He had a fiery red tinge to his cheeks, and I wondered why he was so cross about being photographed. Looking more closely into his eyes, though, I saw sadness, I saw pain. I saw a man whose dreams, despite his hard work and dedication, had yet to manifest.

"Nope, don't know him."

"You're sure?"

"I've never been so sure" was my response (though I had been more sure of other things earlier, multiple times).

She flipped over the page in her notebook and handed me a pen. "Would you be willing to sign here, indicating what you have just told me?"

The page had two columns: Yes and No. There were a number of names under each. I signed under No (I wrote "Miss Trixie Ruffles," the alias I was using at that admittedly less subtle time).

She handed me a peppermint candy and walked away. I decided to end my shopping trip early. When I returned home, my mother asked me how things went, but I decided not to mention this unusual encounter to her.

This morning I had a peppermint, which is what brought this memory to mind.

N

NEMESIS
An Enemy Is Just A Person Who Doesn't Like You Very Much

If there's one thing I really hate it's people pleasers. The phrase itself is unattractive (too many p's, I don't like the way the lips purse when speaking it), and it's undoubtedly used to describe those people whom I, as a person, do not find very pleasing at all.

I blame the parents. They teach children that not only is it alright to aspire to being likeable, it's admirable. This leads them to being kind and thoughtful and, as a consequence, annoying. Nowhere is it written that everyone needs to like you, and in all honesty, it's quite beneficial to have some enemies.

The reason I say this is quite simple. It's because I'm right. The reason I'm right is also relatively simple: having a nemesis means that you are always striving for something, you always have a goal to work towards. Ideally, that goal is being better than your enemy. Realistically, that goal may be destroying your enemy. Whatever. The point is you have a goal.

I myself have had a few nemeses in my life, and each and every one of them served to inspire me to be a better person. Melissa Albright, who suggested that our kindergarten class should line up in alphabetical order rather than based on our parents' income (her parents were socialists). The professor who told me that etiquette at dinner parties was not an appropriate topic for my final essay in his geology course (did he really think I'd stoop so low as to address volcanic eruptions in my treatise?). Lionel Beckonall, the stage manager of my first theatrical production, who dared to imply he knew more about actresses than I (if this were the case, why did I never see him in the company of women outside the theatre?). The editor who felt that the fact that he was in possession of male genitalia meant he was better suited to choose my words (if the public is not familiar with the word fucanaesia, that is <u>their</u> problem, not mine).

If I were to pass any of these people on the street and they blanked me, I would be more than comfortable with this. Their presence in my life served a purpose as, I've no doubt, my presence in theirs did (if only to provide them with the opportunity to tell their children that they were once so near to greatness). I was not put on the Earth to please all people. No one is. Those who try to get all others to love them are in serious need of a boost of self-esteem. As popular as I am, there have been people for whom I am not "their cup of tea." I can only presume they are either jealous of my beauty, talent and/or wit. Or they may just be simple. Regardless, it is of no loss to me -- if anything I use it to my advantage, inspiring me to become even more beautiful, talented and witty (if that were possible).

In many ways, enemies are more important in life than friends. When we cross that finish line in the race of life, we will not run into the arms of those we love. We will turn towards those behind us, those who inspired us to win, and say, "Eat it, losers." That's why life is worth living.

NERVE
Grow A Pair, Why Don't You?

I realise that I am not your "typical" woman. I can't tell you the number of times I've been told that I do things (and not always just in the sack) that no other woman on Earth would dare do. Of course, you could go on and on about the various characteristics that make me unique among females (I shan't stop you if you really want to), but I feel the real explanation lies with my nerve.

Now often times the phrase "You've got some nerve!" is uttered after an obvious act of discourtesy, and as you know, I am a strong believer in manners. I'm referring to being bold, daring, even brazen, if it's necessary to pull out the big guns. Having some chutzpah is an admirable quality. We all have it from birth, but too often we actively work to repress it, and this is a mistake.

In my youth, I briefly worked at a local tourist attraction, the Birthplace of Brockton Field-Boomer, the first openly gay colonel in the Union Army. I was hired as a greeter: I would welcome visitors into the home, point out the cupboard where the Colonel's "private meetings" most frequently took place and encourage donations for the upkeep. However, my intestinal fortitude was soon called upon, when on day three of my employ, there was a ruckus amongst the peacocks kept in the side garden (Field-Boomer adored the species and one of the peahens stationed there was believed to have been a descendant of his favourite bird, "Old Blue Belly").

From the foyer, I could hear Daniel Creamee, the official Peacock Wrangler, shouting for assistance. I left my post forthwith and found Daniel in an indescribable state (though if I were going to describe it the words "covered in blood and plumage" would probably do the job). Pea fowls can be nasty birds; I personally believe they let the iridescence of their upper tail coverts go to their heads and that's why they walk around like they're all that. Needless to say, having seen a situation that needed an intervention, I jumped into action. Within a few moments, I had the birds under control and had spared Daniel's life (though not his job). The director told me he admired my moxie and predicted that it would take me far in life (he was not wrong).

I'm not saying you should risk your life, trying to be a have-a-go hero in dangerous situations. Being bold is not the same as being stupid. But I am saying that what sets me apart from other mere women is that I've got the balls to step up when called upon.

Do you?

NOURISHMENT
The Taste Of An Epicurean

Perhaps one could consider my only failing as a woman is my less-than-stellar ability to cook. While I possess a number of darling teaspoon sets and I do look rather fetching in an apron, I am afraid I was not blessed with the ability to take whatever I find in the pantry, throw it together, garnish it with parsley and serve it to my guests. Luckily, I was blessed with the ability to use a telephone directory and locate another person (generally one born abroad -- if not for the taste then for the accent) who can do such things, and that is why my dinner parties are so exalted in the newspapers' society pages.

Despite my weakness as a *cuisinière*, I simply adore food and consider myself somewhat of an expert. Though I cannot always verbalise it (especially with my mouth full), I notice the subtle distinctions in flavours and appreciate those blends which succeed deliciously. For example, my mouth begins to water (delicately) even now as I recall the exquisite dinner I had last week at Monty's. It was a stew (but came in a small dish as to remove any proletarian connotations) consisting of lamb, beef, pork, chicken, Parma ham, grouse, venison and squid topped with a lonely pod of petits pois. The intermingling of all those scrumptious tastes brought tears to my eyes. After only a few bites, my stomach literally ached with delight.

While I am a gourmand, I am not a glutton, and I do hope the Catholics amongst you will acknowledge the difference. My figure is a literal symbol of the way I've managed all my life to balance my desire for the finer things with my ability to practise self-control. For someone like me, the pleasure I derive from tasting a provocative entree is matched only by the satisfaction I feel when I watch my half-eaten plate being removed from the table. No one should ever finish all the food they have been served for that is quite simply unsightly. Knowing that some poor souls do not have enough to eat should not upset the fragile equilibrium between being a grateful diner and a slop-devouring pig.

Whatever one's cooking abilities or food purchasing power, it is wise to eat slowly and savour every moment of a meal. The divine skill of really tasting food is not the sole territory of the rich. So whatever you tuck into this tea time, be like me and relish every bite. Unless it's relish, of course. Always pass on the relish as anyone who eats that might as well eat shit.

O

OBSCENITY
I Don't Want To Alarm You

This week I have learned a very unpleasant thing about the society in which we are all living in today.

Despite my normally uplifting personality traits, I'm no fool. I know that bread falls butter side down, if you know what I mean. Terrible things exist in the world, but it is not of my nature to harp on about them (as my readers surely know). But this week I discovered something so shocking, so utterly despicable that I feel I must harp on about it, if only to protect some of you more gentle souls from stumbling across this putrescence yourselves as you are checking the latest cricket scores or searching for a cheese scone recipe (which, by the by, you can find in my most recent cookbook, *Recipes My Grandmother Used to Follow Which I Have Altered So That You Can Actually Stomach The Final Results*).

Here is my discovery: someone is using the Internet to display pornographic images. I am sorry to be the one to announce this. The Internet was such a pure place until this person began to corrupt it with dirtiness. What has happened to the world, I ask?

(While I cannot at this time discuss the details of how I came to learn of this, can I at least remind you all that I am not the only woman who wears my brand of stockings? Please don't be fooled by misleading claims -- I am not a reader's wife and my hair colour is naturally and consistently blonde.)

What I really don't understand is how politicians have allowed this to occur. I really thought they believed in freedom. Don't we have the freedom to not have to look at scantily clad ladies manhandling their mammillae or nearly nude men pulling at the backs of their Y fronts? Dear sirs, is that freedom? I pay my taxes, and I would have thought that one of today's leaders' priorities would have been keeping the Internet free of such images. I suppose I am idealistic, but idealism is no bad thing. At least it's not as bad as some of things I've seen online this week.

Oh my. I implore someone to do something to keep cum shots away from the faces of decent, respectable women like me.

Quite frankly, I don't understand why men (for it is they) would like to access such pictures on their computers. Surely, part of the thrill of pornographic material is the public announcement of one's sexual dysfunction through the process of going to some High Street shop, grabbing the offending material in their grubby little hands and completing the transaction in front of innocent shoppers. I don't claim to understand their ways, but I would have thought that private use of this material was besides the point. What on Earth would a man do with pornography in the privacy of his own study or office cubicle? Goodness only knows.

We can do something to combat this growing cancer before it becomes too large to remove without the use of radiation therapy. We must appeal to the Internet's editors; surely they will agree that their names are being tarnished by the publication of smut under their watch. If they refuse to act, we must insist upon their resignation.

The only other thing, I'm afraid, that we can do is be vigilant in our Internet use. I would suggest avoiding the following words when doing Internet searches:

- jiggly
- underpants
- well hung
- twelve incher
- doggy, pussy or horse
- dangle
- lonely
- housewife
- cock

Alas, once again, it falls to the decent people of the world to take responsibility for our own safety. I'm afraid if you can no longer do random searches for "virgins who are gagging for it" without being confronted with some pretty unsavoury results. However, I do believe searches on "becoming a suicide bomber" are still relatively safe.

Be careful, dear ones. You never know across what you might come.

OBSTINACY
Stick It to Yourself

The most interesting man came into my acquaintance this afternoon. His name is B. Huey Hutton, and I would like to introduce him to you, my dear readers. I won't dwell on his physical appearance (not everyone can be blessed in this department, don't forget), but rather on what I did find most attractive about him: his steadfast commitment to his beliefs. Despite the fact that many people see stubbornness as a negative quality and Huey did confess that on numerous occasions he's been called "pig-headed" (I had the good grace not to suggest that the comment may had been directed more at the protuberance between his eyes and mouth), I personally admire those who resolve to stick to their guns. (Point of clarification: Mr Hutton's weapons charge was dismissed before going to trial.) His dedication to his particular stance (in this case, his belief that all liquids should be drunk through straws) is something we could all learn a lot from.

I remember when I was in second grade, I suppose I was a "teacher's pet," but that's only to be expected because of my intelligence and charm. Unfortunately, the principal was concerned that rather than serve as an inspiration to the mediocre children, I would be seen more as an unachievable ideal. Therefore, he requested that my teacher assign me a poor mark. My teacher, bless him, felt that this was undeserving and refused to do so -- damn the consequences! My mother told me that when she saw him years later, he said he never regretted his obstinacy and insisted that he was perfectly happy living at the homeless shelter.

Sadly, our world does not always respect those of us who are committed to our beliefs. But trust me, I do respect that. Each of us has truths that we hold dear to us -- we have moral compasses that tell us right from wrong. Trust yours and hold true to it. If you are in any doubt, ask me what to do; I'll steer you right. I'm good like that.

OVERINDULGENCE
It's Time for an Intervention

If there's one thing I'm getting a little tired of, it's addicts. They get everything these days and I'm sick of it. They've got their own spas, their own music, their own television shows and I'm telling you right now they've got the Christians wrapped around their little fingers.

Now before you start quoting Bill W to me, let me say I know being addicted to alcohol or drugs isn't all it's cracked up to be. Truth be told, it's not the drunks and smackheads that really bother me. In fact, some of my best friends are drunks and smackheads. They're not really the ones I've got my beef with. It's the rest of them -- those addicted to fame, to sex, to Twitter, to collecting crisp packets, to setting fires. Give me a break. The worst thing the medical profession ever did was designate these addictions diseases. Disease, my eye.

It's not a disease that makes people want to get famous and have sex all the time. People want those things because they are fantastically pleasurable (trust a woman who knows). Who wouldn't want to have their photo in the paper or be shagged senseless 24-7? I'm more worried about those who aren't "addicted" to these things. There's something not right there.

If you've never stayed up all night playing online poker or experienced the thrill of throwing a Molotov cocktail into the garage of an ex-lover and watching it burn, baby, burn, then you are missing out on some of life's greatest pleasures. However, if you have done these things and are so greedy that you have to keep doing them, don't try to sugarcoat it with a medical disorder.

When I was growing up, my uncle was a collector of hats. He had a number of them locked away in his special hat room, which children could not enter without first being blindfolded.

Did he have a disease? Was he an addicted to hats? No. He was a well-respected businessman who just liked headwear more than normal people did. No one judged him, but no one took pity on him either.

We all need to start taking a bit more responsibility for the things we do that make us feel good. If you well and truly believe that you don't have control over your desires, be they for love, money or fame, there's a relatively simple solution. Just stop doing them. With a little more thought and effort, it is possible: you just need to accept it for what it is and chill out a bit. In fact, why not have a drink? That always helps to take the edge off.

P

PASSION
Just Don't Frighten The Horses

I was disheartened to hear that an official complaint against me has been filed at my local club. Two gentlemen (I know who they are, but shall keep them nameless for the sake of their unfortunate wives) wrote a letter claiming that my "bawdiness" is throwing our club into disrepute. This is outrageous and, to me, reeks of the sexism that I thought Germaine Greer, Jane Fonda and that lot had completely eliminated.

When I first became an international mover-and-shaker, interviewers would always ask me about making it in a "man's world." Quite honestly, I rarely found that my gender got in the way of any of my achievements (though I did have to bind my chest when I played Tadzio in my college's version of *Death in Venice*). I would say that I have generally been treated as respectfully as the next man (unless the next man is an estate agent).

However, this new specific complaint has made me realize that while, as a woman, I've been accepted as a brilliant writer, worldwide wit and all around *bon vivant*, it's my life as a sexual being which has thrown these boys into a tizzy. Not only is this offensive, it is quite clearly a case of blaming the victim.

Just like I can't help the fact that I was born with XX chromosomes, neither can I help the fact that people of all ages and sexes find me "shag-able." I do try to keep myself physically fit, but honestly it's for health reasons; the fact that I can still turn a head or two is merely one of the unavoidable by-products. My insistence on having my hair styled and wearing only the finest stockings really is work-related -- readers are hardly going to purchase books written by an author who is repulsive and frightful. I am just trying to do my job. One wouldn't criticise a builder for having muscles or a librarian for wearing glasses, now would one?

That said, I actually find it admirable that I can still give rise to bodily pleasures. Too many people, particularly women, find that once they reach a certain age, sexual relations fall to the wayside. That's a real tragedy because, as we all know, the older one gets, the more knowledgeable one becomes about the mysteries of lovemaking. I'm proud to say that my techniques are still coveted by those I meet (or who hear of my triumphs from others). I am not going to hang my head in shame because men get "semis" when I walk down the street. Instead, I wear them as a badge of honour. To me, these partially erect members illustrate that a woman can really have it all: intelligence, fame, respect and an ass off of which you can bounce a quarter.

I don't know what will come of this accusation. I don't want to be dragged into a countersuit, though I do have some interesting details about both men I hope I am not forced to share. I suppose all we can hope is that this serves as a rallying cry to bawdy women everywhere. We need to stand up, sisters, to the sad sacks who try to keep us quiet. Paint your lips, sway your hips and don't be afraid to bed a complete stranger if that's your cup of tea. A woman is by nature a sexual creature; God gave us these bodies and why shouldn't we indulge in a little titillation if we can still get it? Do what you feel like doing, wherever and whenever and however many times you can manage. As long as no one gets hurt, I can't see how anyone will get hurt.

PREPAREDNESS
Survival Of The Wittiest

A man from the US Homeland Security Department told me that there are five basics for surviving any disaster: food, water, shelter, fire and security. Though it was one of the more unusual pick up lines I've been confronted with at that particular dancehall, this man clearly knows "what's what." During the last disaster I personally survived (the last minute cancellation of a romantic engagement due to so-called work commitments), these five things served me well. Christopher cooked me a delectable dinner in my own fabulous kitchen, accompanied by a tall glass of water topped up with whiskey. I then warmed myself in front of the fire I had started with the thoughtless Lothario's letters and felt secure with the fact that, despite this man's supposed dedication to his job, he will never have as healthy a bank balance as I do. Homeland Security really knows what it's talking about.

However, there are a few finer points on disaster survival that I feel are worth mentioning. These again apply to all disasters, natural or otherwise (and by otherwise I mean man-made and by man-made, I mean made by men). So I suppose really these survival tips are geared more towards the ladies, the truly innocent victims of man's inhumanity. They were taught to me by one Daphne d'Ebriété, my first real mentor. A more refined example of a refined woman, you could not ask for. Miss d'Ebriété was in the habit of describing her retiring to her chamber each night as "taking to her death bed." Although this sounds rather ghoulish, it helped her see that each day could be her last and therefore she lived it to the fullest (which may explain her surprising number of arrests for public indecency). I can recall one of the last lessons she passed on to me. She said quite simply, "Agatha, dying can be a real pisser. But if you're prepared, you can help it be that little bit less shit."

Therefore I shall pass on Daphne's advice to you now, in hopes that it will serve you well during the dangerous times in which we are currently living in.

Firstly, a sophisticated woman should never be without a pack of Turkish perfumed cigarettes. Even though smoking regrettably continues to fall out of favour with each new generation, having access to some lovely smelling foreign fags is vital to a girl's survival. Lighting up one of those babies (don't inhale if you insist on being such a pussy about it) and fondling it in your delicate fingers will serve you well in any disaster: the nicotine and injurious toxins that make it smell so pretty are bound to have some kind of positive effect on your nervous system plus its essential sexiness means you will easily be able to seduce your way to the front of the gas mask queue.

Additionally, a woman should know how to set her own hair. Although it is obviously much more enjoyable to have one's do done by someone else (ideally a young man with nicely trimmed fingernails), it's important to be capable of doing it oneself in a pinch. There are two reasons for this. After the apocalypse, we have no idea how difficult it might be to book a spa appointment, but global catastrophe is never an excuse for looking bedraggled. More importantly, though, the tools of the hairstyling trade may be helpful post-Armageddon: a hot iron will help with making cheese toasties, a barrette can keep your dress from exposing too much thigh and a hair pin could be useful in picking out those pesky chards of glass from your tender flesh.

Finally, it's helpful to always pack a piece.

Following Daphne's advice has kept me alive and kicking for these many years, and I encourage you to take her words to heart. Tomorrow, we may face a disaster of epic proportions and if you don't take heed and you end up dead, well, just don't come crying to me about it.

Sleep tight, dear ones!

PRESENCE
What You Give To The World

I'm often asked how I can simultaneously be on top of things in both the United States and Great Britain, as well as get involved in important developments in other less important countries. I will confess, it's not easy. It really takes it out of a person to be the go-to-girl about current political and cultural events all over the globe. However, it's the burden I've been asked to carry as an international mover-and-shaker, and I carry it with pride in my handy canvas tote bag.

However, even you less extraordinary people can spread the impact of your presence (though undeniably not as influentially as I) with a little effort on your part. Communication is key. I'm presuming that you are already involved in your local community (all members of my fan club are required to sign a "I am not a lazy tosspot" clause), but don't stop there. With the Internet, it's possible to reach out across the globe to keep your finger on the pulse (and your nose poked into) whatever is going down wherever it is going down. Even those not technologically advanced enough to get online can still get knee-deep in others' affairs and engage through good old fashioned post. You'd be surprised at the effect a serious campaign letter writing can have: Winston Churchill first became known through his persistent letters to the editor of *The Times*, promoting leg o' mutton sleeves as a viable fashion statement, and look at the influence on the world he ended up having. Learn everything you can about as much as you can and then get all up in everyone's business.

Perhaps the most obvious way to affect the world, though, is to guarantee that you are ever-present in everyone's hearts. I'm afraid there's no guaranteed quick route to this. I would suggest be good, be wise and, if all else fails, die young in a suspicious car accident in France. It's quite a sacrifice, but it's one way to win the world's affections.

Q

QUALIFICATIONS
Have You Got A License For That?

As discussed earlier, I am indeed a licensed driver in both the United States and the United Kingdom, excluding Cornwall due to a simple misunderstanding that needn't be detailed at present time. To receive said licenses, I, of course, had to go through the normal process of filling out a form, paying a fee and taking a test to prove I was fit for purpose.

Having been initially taught to drive by Grampy Carmichael (whose name was literally the law), there was a part of me that felt the whole charade of a driving test was unnecessary. My evaluator and I were at loggerheads from the get go. He was overly judgmental on my answer to the required depth of tire tread while I found his tie shockingly ugly. Of course, by the end of our little drive, I had received an acceptable grade (though I'm afraid I could only describe his own work as "could do better" after he refused to get out and open the door for me -- manners, my dears, are important and cost nothing). I got the license because I had obeyed by the rules of the law and, after all, the law is the law.

My experience getting my driving license in England was somewhat more trying. I cannot comment on whether the evaluator's piss poor attitude was motivated by strong anti-American sentiment (though it was) or influenced by unspoken sexual tension (which seems to play a role in most of my interactions with the opposite gender). Nonetheless, I eventually passed.

Both of these procedures I was able to tolerate because I wanted to drive, and they were requirements to be allowed a driving license. The laws were put in place to keep the wider community safe. Essentially, any type of license comes with provisions which are designed to keep undesirables away from the public arena.

For example, if you use a licensed taxi, you will know that the driver will undoubtedly behave safely and courteously throughout the ride. We can be assured that no one with a dangerous motive or unhealthy mind will ever get their hands on a gun as these are two qualities which guarantee a license will be denied. In many locations, a man cannot even go fishing or own a dog without first obtaining a license.

This is why I will support any party that proposes a mandatory licensing requirement before couples can reproduce.

For those who argue that this proposal would be the government intruding on our personal lives, allow me to remind you that we are required to obtain a license before we can get married. Although I am proud to say I've resisted the fad of marriage, I have on numerous occasions been engaged and once even made it all the way to the courthouse to apply for a license. After completing the paperwork, a judge called my betrothed and me into his chambers and quite simply stated, "Agatha, I am denying this license on the grounds that this man is not the man for you." Although shocked at his proclamation, I almost immediately realised the truth within it when I noticed that my fiancé had begun to cry. And to think I almost married the man!

The process of applying for a marriage license can keep one from making the biggest mistake of one's life. Applying for a driving or gun license can stop those who can't control themselves from causing a deadly disaster. When I hear the words "biggest mistake of one's life" and "deadly disaster," I naturally think of children. It seems blindingly obvious that no one should be permitted to breed without first taking a test. My goodness, have you seen the kind of trouble unchecked parenting can cause? Head to the City Centre on a Friday evening, and I'm convinced you'll agree that something must be done.

QUIETUDE
I've Got Something To Say About Silence

Most religions honour the concept of silence. The Buddhists practise meditation, sitting quietly for hours on end. The Quakers meet for silent worship and reflection. And Christ knows the Catholics know how to keep their mouths shut about certain things. The reason for this is simple: some quiet time nourishes one's spiritual soul.

A lot of people are afraid of silence, but it can be a great thing. For example, if a man comes up to you on the walk home tonight, announces he's in love with you and gives you a piece of jewellery and/or a wad of cash, you'd be a fool not to stay quiet about your husband and four children at home, let alone the one who's recently been taken into care. Duh. But silence can enhance all our relationships -- not just those with invisible all powerful beings in the sky or fantasy lovers on the street -- even the ones with actual human beings. Yes, it's true!

I can understand your questioning me, because after all, we live in a very loud world. Those who want to get promoted, get richer, or get laid, get louder, not quieter -- watch any reality television show or Prime Minister's Questions to see this in action. So you'd be forgiven for thinking that silence can work against you. Then again, by now you should know that I am more clever than you, so really why would doubt a single word I say? Whatever. I'm over it. I can provide ample evidence for my initial claim and shall do so now.

When your missus came through the door tonight, you knew she had it in for you. (Perhaps the man who proposed his love to her on the walk home had bad taste in jewellery?) The actual reasons are irrelevant; what matters is that you know that within an hour, she's going to have you by the balls over something or other. You could try to head her off at the pass: say something sweet, try to cheer her up and get her on side. That's not going to work, is it?

Firstly, you don't have the slightest idea about how to be sweet, do you? and besides that, she's too cold-hearted to be won over by your feeble attempts at kindness. In a situation like this, there is only one option: silence. From the moment she comes in, keep schtum. Over the course of the evening, she may go ballistic at you or she may turn on the charm or a little bit of both, but you stay quiet. Keep this up until tomorrow morning. You'll be a better man and, if she hasn't left you, she'll respect you for it.

Silence also works a treat with any and all interactions with children. Children love to learn, which is often seen as a good thing, but it also means they love to ask questions to which you are supposed to provide answers. It gets annoying. The next time a tyke comes bounding up to you with a satchel full of queries, give him the silent treatment. Meet his eye or don't, it doesn't matter, just say nothing. What is he going to do -- make you talk? He's a little, helpless child and you're an adult, for god's sake, he can't make you do anything. Say nothing and eventually he'll run off and find another grownup to pester. Sorted.

However, I do want to make one clarification when it comes to the connection between quiet times and romance. A lot of women think they are looking for the "strong, silent type," but this is a myth. When it comes to seduction, silence is deadly. If you are trying to woo a sweetheart, don't let there be a moment's silence. Any dead air is only going to give the person time to realise how much they don't like you. Besides, if you can't think of anything to talk about, are you really that much in love? So keep talking. Constantly. Talk during the cab ride. Talk while you're eating. Keep talking as you're walking home, talk even as you're making your way to the bedroom. Talk all the way through the sex act. Keep talking afterwards. When you're apart, constantly ring them and leave messages, just so they can hear your voice. Avoid silence at all costs. Trust me, they'll love you for it.

In all other situations, though, remember that silence is power. It sets boundaries. If you want to cut someone down or make it to the top, you don't do it by talking sense nor do you do it by shouting your opinions. Silence is more potent than the fists of any anti-war protester. If you want to be heard, don't say a word.

QUIRKS
Yes, I Did That Deliberately

When I was in kindergarten, I was reprimanded for what the principal termed "outrageous behaviour." In addition to having to sit on the bench during three consecutive recess periods, I was sent for a chat with the school psychologist. Not unsurprisingly, I was easily able to turn the tables on him ("What comes to your mind when I say mother?"). I refused to let him shame me. By the end of the discussion, he had to confess that I was indeed "a special little girl."

The truth is we are all special little girls. We are all unique individuals, with quirks and peculiarities. There is no other person on Earth who is exactly like us, which is ultimately a good thing.

Instead of trying to "get to the bottom of" and alter my supposed outrageousness, the school officials should have embraced it (and seriously considered my suggestion that the slower children be used as blockades during tornado drills). Whether our idiosyncrasies are just silly whims or economically viable safety provisions, we should value those things that make us different.

Please understand that I am not supporting the theory that "I'm okay, you're okay." While I am, of course, more than okay, there are plenty of people out there who aren't and who should work to change themselves. But it's rarely their quirks that are the problem.

Perhaps you've been told you hold your pen weird or that your laugh leans towards a cackle. Maybe you look a bit silly when you run or your socks occasionally clash with the rest of your ensemble. You shouldn't have to apologise for these things. In the big picture, they are all part of the rich tapestry of life. Take pride in your oddities. Don't let them distract others or yourself from the real problems you have.

You know what I'm talking about. <u>Those</u> are the things you should be ashamed of.

R

RECOVERY
Hair Of The Dog That Bit You

So you've done it again, eh? Last night, you drank too much, and now you're paying for it.

In the past, you've come to me with your problems and I've helped you, and today will be no different. What you need to understand is that the real issue here is not your hangover, but your feelings. We often get confused about our feelings. We say we love our partners, but if we'd just look a little more closely, what we really feel is hate. We say our friendships are motivated by loyalty, but they're not: it's usually envy (how you may feel towards me) or pity (how I may feel towards you).

So if I asked you now what you were feeling, you probably would describe a headache or tummy upset. Of course, alcohol can eff your body up good and proper, but what are you <u>really</u> feeling? Regret? Shame? Impregnated?

These are the symptoms no hangover cure can help you with. Fortunately, my insight into the true workings of the human body (including the mind) can. Follow these the steps -- to the letter -- and you'll feel better.

Step One
Look yourself in the face (you will probably need a mirror to do so).

Step Two
Notice the regret in your eyes (indicated by a red tinge, drooping eyelids or dark circles).

Step Three
Consider what caused that regret (this may be a specific event or just an acknowledgement of your general failure as a productive human being).

Step Four
Notice the shame on your face (indicated by blotches on the skin, hickeys on the neck or the red itchiness around your mouth as an HSV-1 blister prepares to burst forth).

Step Five
Consider what caused this shame (make a note to call for an STD/pregnancy test on Monday).

Step Six
Comment aloud about how unattractive regret and shame look on you. If you live with someone, get them to tell you you're hideous.

Step Seven
Drink one litre of freshly juiced kale, lemon and garlic (if items are not available -- and they probably won't be because you're not one to plan ahead, are you? -- drink eight ounces of milk that has gone off, which I bet you've got at least a pint of in your fridge).

Step Eight
Vomit.

Step Nine
Splash cold water on your regret- and shame-stamped face.

Step Ten
Get into bed and think about things until you weep yourself to sleep.

I guarantee tomorrow you'll wake up renewed and ready to change your life. Or at least change your sheets.

RESOLUTION
Everyday In Every Way

I have never cared for women named Victoria. I find them repellent. An infant must have some very unappealing traits for her parents to christen her Victoria, when there are so many more clever appellations available.

This is why I feel torn about finding out our local post office may be closing (a woman called Victoria works there). Personally, I'll be very glad to no longer have to cross her path, but in the bigger picture, quite frankly, this announcement is criminal. I know many elderly persons in the village who rely on the post office as the place to buy their cigarettes. Whatever will they do without it?

I suppose many people would give the "sensible" advice of giving up the hideous habit. However, I would suggest a different route: go down the jitty behind the post office and across the park to the other shop which not only sells fags, but also offers some lovely jams made by the ladies of the WI.

Those who suggest refraining from smoking, I'm afraid, are living in a bit of a "dream world." I know it is very popular among some classes to set themselves tasks of giving up habits, especially around the New Year. This is pure tosh. There is no reason to use the excuse of a calendar change to determine one's fate. This doesn't have the take-control-of-one's-own-life-by-grabbing-it-by-the-balls type of gusto I expect from myself and those I admire. Instead I grab my (and, by default, Christopher's) balls every morning by setting New Day's Resolutions: achievements that would better ourselves and the world around us and which can be completed within the twenty-four hour span. This means that every night Christopher and I go to bed a better woman than I was that morning, which may sound hard to believe but is quite simply fact.

Let's look at how this plays out in practice. My resolution for Friday was to be adorable and, despite my late start to the day, I am proud to say I managed to achieve this goal. Saturday I resolved to send out thank you notes, which I did, and today I intend to help another person (which I presume I am doing for you right now). Christopher's resolutions, too, (1. bleed the radiators, 2. sweep the path out front, and 3. find roses for me on a Sunday just because I fancied their smell) have improved him as both a man and a citizen of this great nation. I don't mean to imply that we are better people than those who can only manage one goal a year, but I also am not unaware that evidence shows this to be true.

Never underestimate yourselves when trying to improve your lives. You have the power to do and be anything you'd like. Unless you are called Victoria. If that's the case, I suggest you just give it up now. There's little you can do to make yourself any less revolting so take up a nice quiet hobby and keep your trap shut.

RITES OF PASSAGE
Darling Buds Of May

As we turn over our calendars to expose the new month, we are unsurprisingly greeted with May 1, known as May Day in many cultures. People celebrate it in a variety of ways, but most festivities involve weaving flowers into one's hair, dancing in an inordinately silly manner and/or bashing in the brains of factory bosses. May 1 holds meaning for me as well, though I cannot bring myself to think of it fondly. In my family, May 1 is remembered only as the Day of the Incident.

It began, as so many unhappy stories do, with my mother's Bridge Club. I'm afraid the competition between the women players extended far beyond the card game. The ladies were always trying to outdo each other in their personal lives: a husband's promotion, a son's sporting triumph or an exotic accent belonging to a cleaner -- all were fodder for the rivalry. While often the bragging was greeted simply with patronizing nods, sometimes the afternoons would end with bitter silences and, on one occasion, actual bloodshed.

One Tuesday, something said really set my mother off. It came from the mouth of Deborah Bullwinkle, a relative newcomer to the group, who was married to a dentist whose hygienist's attitude my mother found objectionable. This particular afternoon, Mrs Bullwinkle came in with the story of her daughter's first menstrual period, a tale so fascinating that no one could deny that she had "won" (not at cards, of course -- my mother almost always won at bridge because she is famously a cheat).

When my mother returned home, she was fuming. She began to pick on me: why hadn't I cleaned up my room, swept the back porch or started dinner? She demanded to see my homework, something she rarely did as by then she had realised that my intellectual abilities had surpassed her own. She criticised my

142

handwriting and noted that my dress was wrinkled. This abuse continued until she confessed that what was really upsetting her was the fact that I had yet to shed my uterine lining.

Now when my mother came back from bridge, she was usually pretty loaded so there was no point in trying to introduce any logic into the conversation. At the time, I had yet to reach double digits so my lack of menstruation was hardly my fault. But my mother was determined that I should be able to outdo the Bullwinkles. She then announced that the next day -- May 1 -- I would not be going into school but instead she and I would be heading to Gatsby's Department Store. She would become the first of the Club to buy her daughter a proper, grown up lady's brassiere.

I shan't go into great detail about the excursion, partly because I do not want to frighten my younger readers but also because the clerk has served her time and paid her debt to society. Suffice it to say that my mother was not amused by her suggestion that we start off with a training bra. My mother had not allowed me training wheels for my bicycle when I was learning (as evidenced by the still-visible-today scars on my knees), and "my daughter got her first training bra" would not earn her the respect she was expecting at next week's bridge game. So the clerk, my mother and I bundled into the changing room with a pencil, a pad of paper, and a measuring tape, leaving little space for my dignity.

Ultimately, my mother's bragging about my early entry into the world of intimate apparel gave her the triumph she had hoped for. The fact that my bosom didn't properly fill the cups until quite a few years later was irrelevant. My mother had turned my tender breast buds into a weapon, and it's a testament to my moral fiber that I was able to overcome such trauma and go on to develop the magnificent bustline that I still maintain today.

So this May Day be assured that I'll be remembering the Incident and the hurt that it caused. Whether you're dancing around with ribbons or demonstrating around a bonfire, you know I'd appreciate your taking a moment to think of me. Then, if you aren't already doing so, think of my breasts.

Nice, aren't they?

S

SENSIBILITY
Money And Shoes

As you may well know, older people are full of stories from the past which tend to be tedious and irrelevant to present day. Many a time I have been bored by the old dears going on about the price of potatoes or the prescribed doses of medication "in their day." I try to remember that they are probably lonely now that their own children have forsaken them so I listen patiently until I can get away from them without seeming impolite. Advice is often handed out willy nilly during these ramblings, and I must confess that as many stories as I have heard from the older generation, I have yet to hear a single one as interesting or as informative as my own so this is why I'm delighted to share one with you now.

In my day, dating was simpler and better than it appears to be now. Men and women had clearly defined roles, and it is a crying shame we have strayed so far from these.

Perhaps the greatest lesson my mother ever taught me involved a dime and a shoe. When a gentleman calls for a young woman, if she exits her house unencumbered by a pocketbook or even a pocket, she is saying to her beau, "There is no doubt in my mind that you are man enough to take care of everything this evening." On any date the most important point is to give the impression of full confidence in the other party. Sadly, at the same time, we must also realise that most people are going to let us down. Therefore we should always have a back up plan, and this is where my mother's lesson comes into play. If, for any reason, I had found myself left with a bill I refused to foot or abandoned on a deserted road after an incident while "parking," I would have possessed the needed coinage to phone my parents to come retrieve me and my dignity. By secreting the dime in my shoe, the young boy remained unaware that I had even for a moment considered that the date might go anything but well. This is a wonderful example of forward planning.

Of course, as time moved on, pay phone call charges grew, and it became more uncomfortable to hide three or four coins under my feet. I appreciate today few young people even know what a pay phone is, preferring instead to carry a "mobile" phone with them at all times. I do not think it is coincidence that as mobile phones become more popular, so does divorce. By carrying a mobile phone with her on a first date, a woman says to a man, "One step out of line and I will phone a policeman forthwith." Surely this lack of trust should not exist outside the bonds of marriage.

One note of warning: having heard this story many a time from me, my dear friend Alice Wintergarden kept it in mind when she first dipped her toe back into the dating pool after that unfortunate incident with the retired police officer she met on an encounter weekend. She and a gentleman friend (whose name I cannot recall at this moment but I believe began with a P) agreed to spend the day together. Needless to say, Alice is not vulgar enough to carry a phone on her person. She considered the coin option but was concerned as she was would be wearing open-toed shoes (I would like to point out that I was vehemently against this fashion choice). So she opted to place her debit card under her right foot, hoping that if things were to go unfavourably, she would be able to hire a car to get her home. As it turned out, the morning spent walking in a park was so enjoyable, Alice and her friend decided to prolong their time together by punting down a river. She returned home at an acceptable hour and no doubt went to bed dreaming of her soon-to-be Mr Wintergarden. The next morning she woke to ghastly news. Her current account had been emptied. I am convinced that the pressure of her quite heavy hoof on her debit card had caused the raised numbers of her account to become impressed upon the sole of her foot. She confessed she had removed her shoes while enjoying her time on the river, and this is clearly when the so called gentleman had noticed the numbers, reversed them (because he was that clever), memorised them and used them to his advantage. She insisted that this was not the case and claimed the card itself had gone missing, but I refused to let her see him again. I do not wish to brag, but I am always willing to sacrifice other people's happiness because that is how much I care for my friends.

I beg of you, please take this to heart.

SPIRITUALITY
A Spiritual Journey On The 11.55 To Carlisle

I am all for people choosing their own religion and practising as they see fit. I won't stand in anyone's way of making stupid decisions or absolutely fools of themselves.

I had the opportunity today to speak to someone who's "living the dream" in terms of freedom of religion: a gentle giant who frequents our train station (if you're local, he's the tall chap who wears the mismatched shoes). Big Dave, as I nicknamed him the day he first accosted me, has been accosting me and other travellers for close to three years, hoping to enlighten each and every one. Generally, my response is to smile politely, take whatever pamphlet he's handing out and move on. After all, I too have the right to my own conscience, yes? However, today he said nothing as I passed but instead boarded the train and sat down next to me.

Throughout the ride, Big Dave (whose name I've now learned is actually Colin) showed himself to be a rather interesting and intriguing nutter. He explained to me that as soon as he left school, he realised that he had a spiritual cavern in his life. Naturally, he sought guidance at his local C of E church, but apparently the vicar's voice was like an ice pick through the eardrum so Big Dave moved on to the Methodists. However, he soon discovered an allergy to jam and jumble sales so on a whim, he decided to check out the religious section of the library and had his "mind blown" by the opportunities available there. So essentially since then, he has been taking out books and videos on various religions and sects, learning about their beliefs, histories and rituals.

Admirable, I told him (when I got a chance, because let me tell you, he was quite the talker). He thanked me but admitted that he was greatly concerned that he had now "maxed out" the library's religious selections. He was conflicted as this meant that, until the library purchased some new texts (and who knows when they'll be able to afford to do that, thanks to funding cuts), he was stuck being a Zoroastrian, a religion he wasn't quite sure he understood plus there were relatively few Fire Temples in the immediate region. He confessed that he felt at a spiritual crossroads.

Remembering the UN's Universal Declaration of Human Rights (which is never far from my mind, except while bathing), I advised Big Dave that we have the right to freedom of <u>thought</u>, and if he didn't mind me saying, inhaling books without actually <u>thinking</u> about what they meant, isn't actually taking full advantage of such an important universal human right. Converting to a new religion every 21 days (or slightly more depending on if he remembered to renew in time) was quite charming, but clearly not fulfilling his spiritual needs. Perhaps he should put away the books and just sit quietly (maybe for the duration of our train trip, I suggested) and see where the silence takes him.

I'll be going to London in a few weeks, and I imagine I'll see Big Dave at the station again. I'll be curious to have another chat to learn what's going on with him. It's his human right to practise the religion of his choice; I'm just hoping it's one that satisfies his intellectual and spiritual needs and ideally one that believes cleanliness is next to godliness because I'm pretty sure I also have the right not to have spend two hours on a train, inhaling the smell of piss.

SUPPORT
Mind Your Business

In this day and age, it's difficult for small businesses to survive. Everyday a small shop or local service closes down because large corporations are taking over. Upsettingly, in the US, corporation personhood now exists, where essentially corporations have "rights." This is crazy talk. When I was a child, we were taught to respect those people who set up their own little businesses -- we bought our produce from a farmers' market, we bought our dresses from a local seamstress and the very first cocktail I ever drank was produced by a neighbourhood bootlegger. Small businesses were at the heart of the economy and the community, and I stand behind any campaign that supports them during this difficult time.

That said, if the man who runs the news agent's at the end of my road does not change his attitude sharpish, I will do everything in my power to have his shop shuttered for good.

I am a reasonable woman and a reasonable consumer. I do not make ridiculous demands, and I accept that accidents do happen. I have visited the shop when his stock of Parma Violets was low. Occasionally, the clerk has given me imprecise change. Once, I had to wait nearly a quarter of an hour until the shop re-opened, even though the sign clearly said "Back in 10 minutes." I have never complained about any of these things. Unfortunately, the owner has now taken things too far.

When I woke this morning, I came downstairs to enjoy my cup of tea, boiled eggs and wheat soldiers -- lovingly prepared by Christopher -- as I do every Sunday morning. As he had gone for a boys-only night out last evening, Christopher began to tell me of his adventures. I quickly grew bored and interrupted him to ask for my Sunday papers. This is when Christopher shared with me the devastating news: they had not been delivered. After recovering from the initial shock, I dressed and walked up to the news agent's to see whatever could have been the problem. To be honest, I could only presume that some horrible disaster had occurred. What else could cause the man to have let down a loyal and lovely customer whom he knows relies so strongly on her daily newspapers?

A horrible disaster had occurred, but it wasn't a flood, fire or foul play, but an injustice beyond belief. I was told that the shopkeeper had not received my cheque; therefore, he told the paperboy to cease my delivery. Anyone with any sense knows that I always pay my debts. In fact, this man knows: I have been paying for newspaper delivery the 1st and 15th of every month for as long as I have lived in this village. However, despite my reputation for responsibility, when my payment was not there in his grubby little hands by the end of the most recent due date, he simply crossed my name off the list, as if I weren't a person with hopes and dreams, as if I didn't matter at all. And to add salt to the wound, I had visited the shop yesterday and had chatted with said man. Never once did he utter a word about the state of affairs. Had he done so, it would have taken just a matter of moments to explain that when I realised that I was out of sealing wax, I put a note on the table asking Christopher to purchase some when he dropped by the news agent's to settle my account. When he found out that they did not carry my preferred shade, he went on to another store, neglecting to pay the man.

Perhaps one could argue that Christopher was in the wrong. However, could one not also argue that the shopkeeper's poor selection of sealing wax was ultimately to blame? Regardless, if this man's conduct is indicative of the way other small businesses treat the customers who support them, it's no wonder the world's gone to hell in a hand basket.

T

TOLERANCE
A Wild Garden Can Be A Lovely Garden

Quite an unsettling afternoon at the Garden Club!

Today we were to vote on the first round of the Lovely Garden Competition. We had a record-breaking twenty-three entrants, I'm happy to report. However, the one at the bottom of the Close was described, on its application and by the judges, as a "wild garden," which drew the immediate wrath of the other ladies (and one gentleman) on the committee. The edict was to eliminate it from the contest. I confess, rabble rouser that I am, I felt compelled to question this stance.

I was told that a Lovely Garden must be planned and manicured -- it must be controlled, not wild. When I asked why, one woman nearly fainted with shock and disgust: "Because that is how it always has been! This contest has been running for over fifty years. Those are the rules that we follow, and you know that, Miss Agatha!"

I can relieve your minds that I did not rise to such bait. Instead, I calmly made my case.

"Is it not true, Mrs Tartuffe, that when the Lovely Garden competition started, the Club President banned all gardens that grew Edelweiss?"

"Yes. Mrs Smith's father had been killed in the war, and she was worried about associating with anything German."

"And do you suggest that we begin banning Edelweiss again because anyone growing it is most certainly a Nazi?"

"Don't be silly," she retorted. (Note: I was not unaware that her own garden exhibited said flower.)

"And is it not true that in the 1980s, both bachelors and those who grew pansies were excluded from the competition?"

"I am afraid so," she said, shamefacedly.

"And do you know why?"

"Yes, we all know why."

"And do you suggest that we now exclude any gardeners of the homosexual persuasion?" I knew this would drive home the point as her very own son, a practitioner of man-on-man love, was hoping to take home the blue ribbon this year. Her red face provided her answer.

"So when you look back on the Club's past," I said, "you can see rules or policies that now seem just a little bit ridiculous. My question to you is this: in fifty years, when the Club Competition Committee meets to look at applicants, how will they view our ban on wild gardens? Will they say, yes, that's entirely sensible, or will they see our ignorance and bigotry the same way we see Mrs Smith's or Reverend Lance's? If you do not rate the wild garden, do not award it points. However, should we deny this young man" (who looks quite fetching in his gardening gear) "a chance? Should we deny him his right to participate just because his beliefs about gardens differ from yours? Thinking of those gardeners of the future, which side of history would you prefer to be on?"

I am pleased to say that the wild garden will be considered for this year's honour. Hurrah for our triumph over close-mindedness! And if the young, wild gardener on Blackbird Close is reading this, I would be happy to join you for tea amongst your Tufted Vetch and Creeping Thistle anytime.

TRADITION
The Gee-Gees And Me

It may surprise you to know that I'm interested in the Grand National, as I'm usually rather against events that lead to animals being killed (unless it's very tastefully done). However, today, like most of the nation, I'll be glued to the telly watching the legendary handicap steeplechase run.

When I was an itsy-bitsy girl, my father had an old Army friend we called Uncle Eli. He would spend a few days in our family home, every once in a blue moon. His visits were usually preceded and followed by at least ten days' of silence from my mother, which may explain why I found time with Uncle Eli so enchanting. I thought his excesses were exotic and exciting. Of course, now I find barely functional alcoholics less attractive, but then, a visit with Uncle Eli meant a weekend of well good fun.

One year, my father and Eli invited me to join them on one of their usually private jollies. Though I requested advance knowledge of the details (so I could choose my wardrobe wisely), all Eli would tell me was "You're going to have the time of your life."

And I did. After a quick stop at the one bar in town which also had a children's menu, we drove through the gates of Melvin Purvis Raceway. As soon as we got out of the car, my face was stung by the frenzy that surrounded me. Men of all sizes were frantically running about, holding newspapers, cigars and their wallets as they rushed to the windows and then trackside. While my father and Eli placed their bets, I watched the enclosure through my binoculars.

I was initially seduced by the satiny sheen of the jockeys' silks (I was a child and can be forgiven for this). But soon I was studying the horses. I don't know how anyone can deny the beauty of the equine beast: the muscular curves of the thighs, the seductive shape of the face, the crowning glory of the crest. One in particular caught my eye: a grey colt with a spring in his step and a twinkle in his eyes. I was no expert, of course, but it felt as if that horse was trying to tell me something, and I knew what it was.

I immediately ran to the sides of my adult companions. "Eli," I said, with absolute certainty, "the smart money is on the grey colt, number 27."

My father tried to shush me, but Eli knelt down and said, "What's the scoop, scout? You got some insider information?"

I thought of the way that horse had so boldly stared me down and said, "The information is inside me. I'm telling you, I just know it."

He flipped over the paper he was holding, scanned the page and tutted. "He's being ridden by a bug boy, doll face. Long shot -- 95/1. I don't rate his chances."

I pulled at my pocketbook, emptied all of my resources into my hand and passed it over to him. "Then use my money," I said. "Place the bet."

There must have been something about the tone of my voice or perhaps it was the awkwardness of a grown man being given a child's life savings, but Eli scurried off and did as he had been told. The three of us then made our way to the rails.

"What's his name?" I asked as I went up on my tippie-toes to get the best view.

"Butch Dreams Big" came the answer to my query.

Though the race seemed to only last seconds and the horses passed by me so quickly that the entire field was a blur, I knew what I knew.

"A blanket finish!" I heard a spectator shout. I think I was the only one there who was not surprised when the winner was revealed.

Eli immediately began asking me to pick my favourites in other races, but my father intervened. We collected our winnings (which my father pocketed) and walked silently back to the car. Eli left town the next day, and I was never included in one of their outings again.

The fact that my father did not tell my mother about our adventure made clear to me that, despite my newly discovered talent, my life's meaning would not be found on a racetrack. I have never placed another bet.

The closest I allow myself to come to this forbidden pleasure is watching the Grand National each year. Christopher and I each have a flutter, but the winner gets personal favours rather than monetary rewards. I'm pretty confident about my choice this year, but I shan't share it. If you're betting today, please be sensible.

And good luck to the horses and riders. May you all end your day without bullets in your heads.

TRUST
No Raccoon Has Ever Lied To Me

I've never seen a raccoon in England. If you're not familiar with them, they're furry grey animals with fluffy tails. A bit like squirrels except less squirrel-ish and more raccoon-ish. Their most distinct feature is the black mask across their face, making them look like cuddly bandits. Cute! What I like most about raccoons, though, is that they are incredibly trustworthy.

This may come as a shock to you, but as a child, I lived for eight months in Canada. My mother led me to believe that this location change was due to my father's draft dodging. Alas, I was too young to realise that not only was the draft not enacted at the time, the US was not even at war. Nonetheless, I still see my father as a conscientious objector, and I look back at those months with great fondness.

One day I decided to head out for a long walk in the Canadian wilderness. I went with one of my brothers (or sisters, I don't remember exactly, and does it really matter?). We hiked through the woodland, making small talk and pausing frequently for me to capture nature with my Kodak Instamatic.

It was mid-July. While most of us tend to think of cold when we think of Canada, I can assure you it was well hot. After an hour or so, my brother (or sister) and I were regretting not bringing drinks with us and decided to head home. However, we had lost our way, and neither of us had our compasses. As we were plotting out our plan back to safety, I noticed a little raccoon with her kits. I bent down to take a snap (even in times of danger, I am committed to my work as a documentarian) when I swear the mother stood up on her back legs and beckoned me towards her. I cried out, and she and her babes scuttled off. We ran over to where the raccoons had been and spelled out on the ground with pebbles was the word "wow."

"What do you think it means?" my puzzled sibling asked me.

I walked slowly around the message. From a different angle, it spelled out "mom." So I determined that the raccoon was either directing us towards something worth seeing or leading us to our mother. Either way, we decided to follow and took off in the direction in which the animals had fled.

We quickly caught up with the raccoon family, primarily because they had thoughtfully stopped to wait for us. Again the mother used her little paw to urge us forward. As we made our way through the trees, we began to hear the sounds of a waterfall and then of gleeful laughter. We were almost home safe!

As we rounded a corner, though, it quickly became clear that we were not at the Whitt-Wellington homestead but rather the raccoon had led us to a park for nudists. My brother (or sister, whatever) and I stood transfixed as we watched the nudie grownups frolicking in the water, lying in the sun and bending over to pick flowers. For a few moments, we were frozen in our tracks. Then, we turned our heads away from the spectacle and saw the raccoons were off running, so we followed again for quite some time until we ended up behind a police station. We went in, our folks were rung, and eventually we got home. Neither my sibling nor I mentioned the nudists to the cops, our parents or each other. That day I learned what a naked man looks like, and all I could say was "wow" (read whatever tone you want into that). The other thing I learned was that raccoons can be trusted.

I bring this up because we are coming up to February 2, also known as Groundhog Day in America. In Pennsylvania, a whole bunch of people get together to listen to a groundhog called Punxsutawney Phil predict the weather. (If you're not familiar with what groundhogs look like, it's nothing like raccoons.) If Phil sees his shadow, it means six more weeks of winter; if he doesn't see his shadow, an early spring is coming. The problem is, of course, that groundhogs are notorious liars, and Phil's predictions are usually wrong.

Don't go to groundhogs for your information. If you want to know the weather, simply look out your window. However, if what you want is the truth -- regardless of how harsh, wrinkly or dangly it might be -- a raccoon will lead you to it.

U

UGLINESS
The Good Are Good -- The Bad, Frightfully Ugly

As I was born with a charitable nature, all my life I have sought to help those in need. I unselfishly give away the many unwanted gifts I receive each year to local charity shops to help increase their revenue. I have donated my time to teach underprivileged children to read, offering up copies of my own books to them at an extremely generously reduced cost. I have traveled to faraway countries to help literally build new communities, and I can tell you there is nothing more rewarding than being present while someone christens a new sewer system. I buy a new poppy every single year, and I have no qualms about telling other shoppers in the queue at Sainsbury's to shut the hell up if we happen to be waiting together at eleven on Remembrance Day. I do these things not so I can then brag about them during lectures to the WI or to you, my devoted readers. I do them because frankly that is just my nature: there's no two ways about it, I am a good person.

Alas, we good people are becoming few and far between these days. I don't want to seem overly moralistic here, because I am aware that good people sometimes do bad things and that being bad once doesn't necessarily make one a bad person. As you know, I do not believe in unfairly judging people.

At the same time, though, people seem to be up to some real evil-doing these days. I'm dismayed by the crimes of all natures which I read about in the papers and the stupid choices politicians around the world seem to be making. Even in my own village, I witness my neighbour leaving his dog in his back garden all night, despite the cold and horrendous noises the creature makes, and let's not forget about the dressmaker who not only delayed the delivery of a dress by six days but when said dress was delivered, it clearly fell three inches below the owner's knee as opposed to the two inches that had been requested. Ugly, ugly.

Can we really say that these are simply "bad acts" and not "bad people"? No. I think it's high time we stand up and call a spade a shovel.

It used to be that those of us who were good were the norm; the bad people were a minority group easily identified by their tendency to drink straight from the bottle or that ever-present evil glint in their eye. Today, though, they are more difficult to spot. Therefore, I have devised a quick test to determine where each of us stands. Firstly, I ask that you yourselves complete this straight forward assessment; you never know, you might actually be a bad person who is just so good at being bad that you have in fact fooled even yourself. You may then want to pass this out to those you come into contact with (especially those with whom you do financial or sexual trade). It is a simple way to separate the wheat from the chaff.

1. *If you were angry with the woman who lived next door to you, would you:*

> a. Beat her with a lead pipe and bury her behind the shed before you went through her bungalow, snatching anything that looked like it might be of value on the black market.
> b. Complain about her loudly to both the postman and the woman who lives across the lane.
> c. Paint a rude symbol on the pavement in front of her house.
> d. Think to yourself, seeing as how she is an internationally famous writer and the highlight of your life is watching *Countdown* each day, perhaps she was right about it being your responsibility to maintain the creosote on the fence.

2. *If you worked at a bank and a woman came in wanting to change her collection of two pound coins for newer, shinier two pound coins, would you:*

> a. Throw the bag of coins in her face, bruising her delicately rouged cheeks.

b. Point out to her that it is midday and the bank is very full of customers whose needs are apparently more important than hers.

c. Close your window.

d. Meet her request because it is nice to see someone who appreciates the aesthetic as well as monetary value of Her Royal Majesty's mint.

3. *If you lived in a small village and had a son or daughter under the age of sixteen, would you:*

a. Feel comfortable allowing your child to enter the local shop without your own personal supervision.

b. Grant your child the privilege of riding a scooter, skateboard or public transport through the village.

c. Permit your child to call any adult by their Christian name.

d. Teach the kid to mind their manners and keep the hell away from my hydrangea.

Clearly, if you answered anything other than d, you are a bad person. The facts speak for themselves. While I do feel sorry for you because you haven't experienced the grace and beauty that comes with being good, I think it is probably more important for everyone that you get yourself together pronto and consider relocating because I can tell you right now, my friend, I am going nowhere.

UNDERSTANDING
Don't Say You Do If You Don't

I've always really fancied men who wear spectacles. It's not that I assume they're brainiacs (usually they're not) or because I believe that old maxim that men who are long-sighted are long in other departments as well. It's quite simply because one of my first gentleman callers wore eyeglasses, and I've always held a soft place in my heart (and sometimes elsewhere) for him.

His name was Langston DeSquid, and the way his strawberry hair fell gently onto his tortoise shell frames was deliciously addictive. I'd watch the glasses slide down his handsome nose and be laid down on the table when he took them off to rub his baby bear brown eyes. However, we had incredibly different ideas about our affiliation. We were equally enamoured, but he wanted it to lead to a more traditional coupling (monogamy, marriage, blah blah blah). I did not. This caused me to be rather defensive at times, which led to disagreements of a monumental scale.

One afternoon (and I remember this clearly even though at the time I was quite drunk), our bickering had turned into a set-to bordering on a ruckus until I proposed a trial separation. Langston was adamantly against this. I lamented, "But I'll never understand you and you'll never understand me. It will never work." Langston took my hand and explained, "Dearest Agatha, there is a difference between understanding and tolerating. You are right: I don't understand why you refuse to be my wife and I never will, given my impressive bank account and skillful lovemaking. But I know that's how you feel and I don't have to understand it, I just have to tolerate it." These wise words were eye opening for me. Sadly, when he decided to quit his job and "get the old band together," I'm afraid I could neither understand nor tolerate, and we parted way.

Of course, there are differences that one should try to understand. We all have lived our own experiences and have our own perspectives on those experiences. Sometimes it's good to try to understand a different viewpoint.

However, Langston's message is important. Whether in romance, business or politics, many people strive to always understand their opponent's positions. This can be a colossal waste of time. Some things are beyond reasonable people's understanding. Who could truly understand why a man would wear a handlebar moustache, why a woman who is a total idiot thinks she should be President of the United States or why anyone would still go line dancing? It would take a sick mind to truly understand that, and I refuse to voluntarily put my own mental health at risk. However, these people do exist, and it's no use pretending they don't. Therefore we have to tolerate their existence. But we needn't try to understand them, in the true sense of the word. So many people beat their heads against the wall trying to comprehend the incomprehensible.

When you find yourself at loggerheads with someone, have a good think. If you're confident that you're a sane person (a certificate can be obtained as assurance) and you still can't get your head around their ideas, it might be time to stop trying. All you need to do is tolerate the person's existence and try to cling to the memory of their lovely, lovely spectacles.

UPBRINGING
Everything My Mother Did Was Wrong

As I may have mentioned every single time I meet a man, I do not have children and rarely intend to.

One look at my figure may lead you to assume it is why I have remained without the burden of offspring. However, the real reason, if I'm frank, is that I have witnessed what poor childrearing skills can do to a delicate little one, and I swore I would never inflict that trauma on another human being (or at least on human beings under the age of fourteen).

Far be it from me to claim that I know the best things to do to raise a child, but what I do know is what <u>not</u> to do, and unfortunately my mother did those things in spades. So let me pass on some lessons you can learn from a couple of her stunts. (You may want to sit down for this, and please please please do not contact the Trenton Child Services Department, however moved to do so you might be. What's done is done.)

1. *Do not put your own needs before your daughter's*
Whether she requires food, shelter, medical treatment or four (not three) cases of imported soda for her birthday party, a child should not have to make such sacrifices just because you haven't budgeted well.

2. *Children need encouragement*
If a strange man at a gas station starts up a conversation with you about wanting to make your daughter a star, don't be so quick to say no and threaten to ring the police.

3. *Consider carefully everything you say to your child*
If you make a comment like "I didn't dirty that dish so I'm not going to wash it," it may come back to haunt you one day once she's taken on the responsibility of doing chores.

4. *Once your child is old enough to get a driving license, for God's sake, upgrade your vehicle*
Bullying is rife at schools, and you are putting your child's safety and more importantly reputation in jeopardy by making her drive a station wagon.

5. *Do not try to turn your daughter in a smaller-boned version of you*
Take a look at your life -- she deserves better than that.

Now these lessons may seem obvious to those of us with even one sensible bone in our bodies, but perhaps some hormonal release once adults become parents makes it hard for them to grasp. I don't know because, as I've said, I've never had children. However, be aware that everything you do will have consequences. Why not make them happy consequences rather than ones that lead to initially a lengthy spell in psychoanalysis and eventually to a bitterness that requires your daughter to discuss publicly your failings as a parent at every opportunity she gets?

Perhaps I should thank my mother, because clearly all her mistakes have shaped me and turned me into the almost perfect woman I am. However, I can't. So I won't.

V

VERACITY
I Rarely Sleep With Liars

I'm not one to fall for silly lines. I can't count the times I've been told I was the "first" or the "only true" or the "most bendable" love a man has had, and I have always seen right through his strategy. Men are often confused by what they see as women's unrelenting commitment to truth. Of course, truth is important to women, as it should be for all right-minded people regardless of the layout of their pubic areas.

But truth is a complicated concept, and a brief explanation of the nuances between the different kinds of truth is warranted.

The Whole Truth And Nothing But The Truth
No one wants this. It's too ugly. Although witnesses in court cases are threatened with a needle in the eye, neither the prosecuting nor defense tables really want anyone telling the whole truth. The last time you waterboarded someone, you probably asked them to tell you the whole truth. What if their truth was actually "I will say whatever you want me to say to get you to stop doing this"? You'd look a fool. Anyone with a lick of sense can see that this kind of truth isn't helpful to any romantic or military conflict.

Lies, Damned Lies
Now obviously this route is neither correct nor seemly. We all know this: telling one lie leads to another lie and another and then it's a pack of them. Not only is it horrible, but it's also very difficult to keep track of. It's one of the great lessons of childhood -- remember the itsy bitsy spider who weaved the web of lies because she was practising to deceive the old woman who swallowed the fly? Your grandmother didn't tell you that story for nothing, you know.

The Facts But Not The Details
Generally, this is the appropriate level of truth for almost all

situations. Details do one of two things: hurt another person or make you look like a twat. An appropriate fact would be "Yes, I saw the defendant hanging around the office building"; there's no reason to add "so I invited him in and gave a passkey to the safe." It's a subtle balance, and you'll often be pressed to give as many details as you can, but resist.

Let's look at a couple typical scenarios men and women find themselves in which the "truth" can play a key role.

Do I look fat in this?

> Don't say: "Yes, you look fatter than I've ever seen you. Take off the offending item immediately and hide your shame. You shall not be attending the ball with me tonight."
>
> Don't say: "What on earth are you talking about? You look so thin I feel compelled to force feed you" (if she actually does look like this, immediately get her to a medical professional).
>
> Do say: "It shows off the real you, and that's the you I love."

Did you cheat on me with that woman?

> Don't say: "I did, and it was the most fantastic shag of my life, partly because of the illicit nature of the encounter and partly because she let me do that thing you said you'd die before letting me do again. Therefore I intend to keep seeing her, but I don't see any reason to let my cheating change our relationship at all, so would you make me a sandwich, please?"
>
> Don't say: "I don't know what you are talking about. Someone has clearly altered that picture to make it appear I'm having sex with her in my dental chair afterhours when I claimed I was away at an orthodontist convention."
>
> Do say: "I did because I am a small man in more ways than one. If you forgive me, I'll be forever indebted, but I'll also understand if you change your relationships

status to 'It's Complicated' and get new locks on the house."

Of course, the easiest way to deal with the truth is to take a little care in advance. If you're about to do something that one day you may need to tell a lie about, the most sensible approach is just not to do it. Don't take the money from the till. Don't text a photo of your erection. Don't marry a fat woman. It isn't too difficult to understand.

But men are fallible creatures and seem to get themselves into troublesome situations at the drop of a hat. You're welcome for my helpful advice.

VIGILANCE
Crime Prevention Tips

I've decided to offer some of my crime prevention suggestions to you, my loyal readers, free of charge. Please do not assume that these suggestions aren't as valuable as the ones I've given in lectures in years past (where the organisers have generally asked for a small monetary donation): it's just that here you don't get biscuits. Go grab yourself some if you feel they're needed for you to be able to pay attention.

I only mention that I'm offering this advice *gratis* to highlight that, sadly, there is a smorgasbord of scammers and dodgy dealers just waiting to relieve you of your hard-earned cash. This is my first tip: be wary of everyone. Now you know me, you trust me, because I'm very likeable, honest and always leave my clientele satisfied, if you know what I mean. So were I to request a small fee, it would be sensible to pay it. However, how many times do you hand over your coins or credit cards to people whom you do not know, admire or find sexually alluring? Just bought your wife a necklace -- are you sure the jeweller isn't in the blood diamond trade? Found a great deal online -- how reputable is the company? The donation you made outside the Post Office -- was the fact that the man owned a red bucket all you needed to hand over a tenner? I'm certainly not saying that you shouldn't buy things from retailers or give money to charities. I'm just saying if you're going to be mindless about how you throw your money about, don't come whining to me about being ripped off. And if you are financially supporting corrupt companies and practices, then in many ways you're just as bad as the criminals themselves. What are you going to do next, kill a fluffy kitten just to watch it die? You disgust me.

Another crime to watch out for is pickpocketing. People get so wrapped up in how many errands they have to run or how many purchases they have to make that they let their guards down. They focus on their lists or rushing to beat the queues, and they leave their purses or pockets easily accessible to baddies. My tip to avoid those with sticky fingers is to keep your wallet hidden upon (but not within) your person. Women are advised to keep their cash in their brassieres; men should tuck it discreetly into the pockets of their Y-fronts. Yes, it may be uncomfortable and possibly awkward at the till, but it's safer, and safety don't come easy, baby. I do <u>not</u>, though, recommend this technique when shopping in toy stores, for obvious reason.

Break-ins are also making a comeback. It's best to assume that burglars are constantly staking out your home. They're watching you carry bundles of purchases from your car, they take note of the empty boxes you put out with the recycling, they know when you're packing the car to go away for a few days. The only way to deal with this threat is to beat them at their own game. Be sensible when displaying new and expensive items you're bringing into the house; use security lighting outside your home; cancel milk and post delivery, set timers or hire a housesitter if you're going away; devise a schedule which means a family member is sitting guard at all entry points to your house 24-7. Don't be a passive victim. Getting robbed is terrible, but it stings even more if you could have proactively avoided it.

Lastly, it's important to remember that even those you love are capable of committing the most horrendous crimes against you. For example, parties involving friends or family often include the imbibing of excess amounts of alcohol-based concoctions. As statistics show, when people drink too much, they are more likely to become aggressive which can lead to cruelty, violence and property damage. My tip for avoiding any trips to hospital and/or the local police station is to water down Granny's sherry from the get go and confiscate both her cane and knitting needles upon arrival.

It is important to keep in mind, though, that baddies do exist, and if they've got you in their sights, there's probably little you can actually do to prevent the inevitable.

VOICE
Let No One Speak For You

One skill I am blessed to possess is the ability to really <u>know</u> someone simply by hearing their voice. Call it women's intuition, a deep understanding of human psychology, my worldly knowledge -- whatever, I don't really care what you say. I'm more interested in how you say it.

There are three things that contribute to the sound of our voice: our physiology, our environment and our attitudes. Physical features such as our muscles, lungs, teeth, tongue and lips all contribute to the pitch and tone of what comes out of our mouths. Now there's not a lot we can do about those things: we get what we're born with and I certainly don't support any of the drastic measures some have gone to to try to change their voices, such as vocal cord surgery, tooth removal or cessation of a forty-a-day smoking habit. That's craziness.

Our environment gives us our language as well as our accents. People's reactions to and assumptions about these different sounds depend more on the listener than the speaker. Some feel the French language is essentially sexual; some think a Kentucky dialect indicates stupidity; some believe a Welsh accent means a person has engaged in relations with sheep. I won't deny that there are some speakers whom I think sound quite silly, but I'm sure there are people who feel the same about me (though objectively they are obviously incorrect). I was quite surprised to find how rife accent bigotry is in the UK when I first arrived, especially as I find all of the ones I hear here delightfully compelling. Doubtless, there are languages and accents that I enjoy more than others, which is my right so get off my back. But in general, what I learn from a person's accent is only from where they come. Their use of language, on the other hand, might tell me something about their education or thinking skills, but each must be judged individually without reliance on stereotype. Even Australians are wise enough to know that.

Now if you are an actor, a world traveller or a criminal on the lam, you may be tempted to try to learn a new language or change your accent. I shan't argue against this; however, I do warn that it's much harder than it appears. While some peeps are genuinely multilingual and many impressionists are extremely talented, witness the debate about John F Kennedy's jelly doughnut status or the offense of Dick Van Dyke's Cockney attempt. I would like to offer just one word of suggestion to those English people attempting to speak "American": when you've got a word that ends in a vowel, don't add an R after it. I don't know why you do this -- most Americans don't -- and it really bugs the shit out of me.

The one aspect of our voice that we can easily control is our attitude. As our attitudes are part of our personalities, sadly many people are too bullheaded to be willing to take a good look at themselves and see what's not working. It's worth noting, though, that if people grimace when they hear your voice, you've probably got some room for improvement.

Lots of people claim that they no longer have a voice these days, but this is clearly baloney. Try saying your name aloud: there you go, that's your voice! Everyone can talk except those who can't, so speak up and let me at you. I'll tell you something about your background and your character and for an extra dollar, I'll guess your weight as well.

Roll up! Roll up!

W

WISDOM
Let's Just Have A Think About That

Few of us truly understand how directly beliefs can affect the spiritual, emotional and physical health of ourselves and our world. Sometimes this is positive; for example, one might believe that her experiences as an international mover-and-shaker are interesting enough to share in books. Those books are then read worldwide and make even the lowliest of people stop before swallowing the whole bottle of pills, promising to dedicate their lives to being more fabulous, which then improves the entire global community. However, things don't always go so nicely. A person might believe that those without enormous trust funds don't deserve basic human rights and then do his level best to fuck up the lives of others once he becomes an elected official.

Since what we believe has power, it's important to think critically about what we think about whatever we're thinking about. Too often we just follow along with the ideas our friends and family, the media or taxi drivers pass on to us. We easily buy into what are called "commonly held" beliefs without ever questioning them, and that'll end up leading to nothing but trouble: from small hassles within our own households to devastating world wars and natural catastrophes. It takes time and energy to think critically, of course, but as usual, I'm here to help. Let's debunk a few assumptions that most people seem to just take for granted as truth and examine their possible consequences.

An apple a day keeps the doctor away
There's no need to worry about doctors showing up at your house unnecessarily: most doctors don't make house calls, so if you really don't want to see one, just don't go into the surgery. Of course, apples are tasty and good to eat, but we need to stop perpetuating the fear of doctors stalking our homes because it scares little children who sometimes have to walk past hospitals on their way to school.

Breaking a mirror means seven years of bad luck
A mirror is simply a fancy pants piece of glass that reflects whatever you put in front of it. Breaking a mirror has no more negative affect that breaking a champagne flute: if you step on a piece, you could cut your foot but other than that, it's no biggie. If you're really worried about seven years bad luck, avoid getting married.

Waking a sleepwalker could be dangerous
First off, sleepwalking doesn't exist: the person is pretending. Why do you think you always find your husband "sleepwalking" his way to the whorehouse? The next time you encounter a sleepwalker, throw a lit match at them and you'll see how quickly "waking" one can actually prevent a dangerous situation.

Dropping a penny from the Empire State Building can kill a person
This belief encourages people to throw away their money and perhaps without it, the economy would be in better shape. If you want to kill a person on the sidewalk below, the best bet is to drop a bullet out of gun while aiming it at their head.

Goldfish have a two second memory span
Why do you even care? What are you doing to your goldfish that is making you obsess over how well they remember things? The truth is goldfish have wonderful memories -- I personally have met goldfish who can remember the Korean War in great detail so just watch yourself.

Eating a dictionary can improve your vocabulary
The ink used in dictionaries can stain one's teeth and cannot be properly processed by a human's digestive system. To improve your vocabulary, read more books and do more crosswords.

Unfortunately, I can't always be there with you and if I have ever promised to be, I'm guessing I was probably drunk at the time. Please use these examples as models to question all of your beliefs. Hold tight to the solid, helpful ones and dump the others. Many local communities have salvage centres where you can drop off dumb ideas that can be recycled into jewellery and household goods which can then be sold on Etsy.

WORDS
On Keeping One's Head

Scientific research produces many lessons every single day that could help humanity become wiser, safer and healthier. The scientists' mistake, I'm afraid, is releasing that information to the public. Most people are just a little too short on technical mumbo-jumbo to be able to interpret complicated scientific reports. For example, remember when a scientific journal announced that "humans should avoid consuming antifreeze"? Sadly, I'm afraid you'll find that coolant-related deaths skyrocketed the very next day. Worse yet are the marketing executives with their so-called suits and ties who manipulate scientific information to use it to sell products. I personally find very dubious products which claim scientific proof that they will remove more stains from my delicates, put hair on my chest or are ribbed for my pleasure. Poppycock!

Instead I have learned all I need to know from the homespun science of my dear Granny Wellington. Boots, as we used to call her, spread health advice like the plague, and I truly believe she is the reason that even to this day I can run six miles (though I choose not to), climb up ladders to clean out my gutters (which I would do, but Christopher seems to enjoy it so) and catch the eyes of men significantly younger than I (a lady never kisses and tells).

Boots explained that our brains are muscles, and to keep muscles strong, we must exercise them. We need to really keep them oiled, work them, flex, pump and drill them, over and over, until they almost can't take the exertion and then stop just short of any actual explosion, even when they beg for more. That is why both Boots and I are great fans of crosswords.

Crosswords are beneficial in many ways. They help improve our memories by requiring us to recall incredibly useless words that we may once have overheard from someone else's conversation in a library commons room or on public transport. (Thank you to the toothless woman who unknowingly introduced me to the term hoose.) They encourage us to keep learning and improving our vocabulary when we find ourselves scanning the OED for an eight letter word starting with st, ending in t and meaning the opposite of crooked. The puzzles also simply keep our minds occupied when otherwise they may obsessively worrying over whatever trifling crises we think we are experiencing. Surely it is a better use of a time to be filling in little boxes on newspaper print than being concerned about a parent's drug addiction, planning for our retirement or finally making an appointment to have that tumour checked.

By doing a crossword, you are saying to those around you, "I know my stuff" or "I'm no dum-dum" or "I am simply waiting for the train and do not wish to be bothered by the likes of you." You are telling people that you respect cleverness, big words not that many people know as well as dictionary compilers, three things which are not held in as high esteem as they should be.

So grab your thesaurus, open the broadsheet of your choice and crobunclivate your heart out. I promise your brain will thank and you'll never feel "2 down"!

WORK
Work Makes You Many Things But Free Isn't One of Them

As my father used to say, "If work was supposed to be fun, it'd be called fun. Work is work, that's why it's called work." Gertrude Stein he wasn't, but he does make a valid point. So many people today think that success in their careers will lead to happiness. I'm afraid that kind of attitude is going to lead to nothing but disappointment (and premature damage to the respiratory and cardiovascular systems). Very few people can truly say that their work makes them happy. Luckily, I am one of those few. But the rest of the world goes to work, not out of love for their job or compassion for their colleagues or customers, but rather simply for the money.

Ultimately, the problem lies in the nature of employer-employee relations. I don't have the time or energy here to rehash what was so thoughtfully explained by our dear friend Pierre-Joseph Proudhon. The gist of it is this: if you're the employee, you're nothing. You will never satisfy your boss; he will never think you give enough. You might have the highest sales figures or land the biggest contract or reach the top of the best-sellers list (for each of your last eleven publications), but he is never going to stop pushing you, pulling you, sucking you dry. He's The Man, and that's how the Man rolls. You're fooling yourself if you think you'll ever be able to overcome this power dynamic. So just stop that silliness right now.

The only thing you can control in a work environment is your approach to your job. So keep two things in mind at all times. First, remember that work is never enjoyable. Everyday you will wake to your alarm, leave your home and head into a fucking nightmare. It might be your line manager blaming you for his mistake, the woman in the next cubicle who smacks her gum, the customer who wants his money back because he didn't lose the twenty pounds in twenty minutes as your advertising guaranteed he would -- whatever it is, it's going to be horrible. If someone is kind to you, assume it's a trick. You're better off expecting the worst and being pleasantly surprised that you're not emotionally and physically destroyed by home time.

Secondly, maintain a cool distance between you and your job at all times. Don't give out personal information to anyone at work, not even the mail boy you had a fumble with at the last Christmas do. Never call your boss by her first name. Do not sign birthday cards or contribute to going away gifts. When the receptionist goes into anaphylactic shock after accidentally swallowing a peanut, just walk away. Showing that you care about any task, person or responsibility related to work is as good as admitting you're beat. You might as well bend over, drop trou and let The Man stick it to you.

Keeping these two things in mind will make the experience of work tolerable enough to make it to just one more payday or until you finally hit it big at Foxy Bingo.

When that day comes and you are able to bid a fond farewell to your beloved employer, remember not to let your guard down. Often we find ourselves looking back at our time with a certain company with fondness, once we know we are leaving. This is a mistake. Remember, you were nothing to that company when you worked there, and you're even more nothing now that you're going. A dear friend who is moving on to bigger and better things recently asked me for some advice on writing his resignation letter. He showed me a few drafts he had spent half the night working on, trying to strike the right balance between expressing his appreciation and saying his piece over various grievances. I tore these drafts up in front of his stupid face and sat down and penned this for him (names have been changed to protect the weasels):

Dear Sir,

It is with much regret that I am writing to inform you of my resignation.

When I say "much regret," of course, I mean "with slight trepidation," as I am hoping this letter will not lead to any kind of interaction between you and me, beyond the usual meaningless drivel we already share. In fact, this letter need not be acknowledged or discussed in any way. On my final day of work, I will be happy to delete the pornography from my computer, empty my desk and walk away from your life forever. I prefer this company think of me and my time here as if it were a dream -- not the best of dreams, not a nightmare, but something in between -- a strange but intriguing time where things didn't really make sense but, in the end, didn't really have to.

If you do, however, feel compelled to discuss this issue further, please be aware that I do not intend to bite my tongue about my experiences here. For example, do you remember the woman who invented "The Alastair," the solar powered vibrator you were convinced she had named after you? The morning after I shagged her, I told her you thought that and she laughed so hard I had to shag her again to stop her from becoming hysterical. Also, if you force me to, I will confess that Phil is the one who's been pissing in the sinks and that the missing supplies from the stationery cupboard can all be located in Daniel's lower intestine as he suffers from an inexplicable urge to eat cello-tape. Matt did not earn a degree from Bournemouth; his flat mate (a hobo) is good at both designing fake certificates and writing recommendation letters. Finally, it was James who bought you the inappropriate Secret Santa gift last year; you think he admires you for your design skills but it's really your arse he is coveting.

I am quite sure neither one of us really wants me to have to share this information. Therefore, why don't we considered this matter closed?

Sincerely,

The One You Insist on Calling Roger, Even Though My Name is Robert

I've no doubt that when he handed in this letter, Robert's boss was secretly impressed with his coolness towards a company that had employed him for over twenty five years. In fact, I am convinced the suit against him will be dismissed before ever making it to court. He stood firm, calm and collected, and that's to be admired.

We've all got to work (and by we I mean you), so accept it for what it is: a means to an end. Every morning you go, you do what needs to be done, you cash your cheque and that's all there is to it. It's not fun, it's not fulfilling. It's a job. That's it.

X, Y, Z

Obviously there is nothing worthy of note that begins with the letter X. Grow up.

YOUTH
Hobbies, Not Just For Horses

The longer days, brighter sun and warmer temperatures (at least theoretically) mean many things, only one of which I'll be discussing today. Semesters are wrapping up, terms will soon be ending and we will be faced with the annual deluge of children with little to do and my neighbourhood to do it in.

I'm not here to argue for more government funding for activities for children; I'm no fool. Pleas for reason clearly fall on deaf ears when the brains in between them aren't bright enough to see the importance of funding schools and children's health care. Trying to get cash for a skate park seems a bit daft. So instead I am directing this to parents themselves: focus on your own children, meet up with other parents and work it out together. It's not that I advocate embracing the concept of the Big Society, but let's face it, politicians aren't doing jack to help.

Therefore, the starting point is to introduce hobbies that keep young people interested and away from my front gate. A good hobby is beneficial to each of us -- it can keep us healthy, productive and happy. Through my own research, I have determined that the most popular hobbies of youth today include swearing, spitting and pulling up their trousers. Unfortunately, these hobbies are <u>not</u> good ones.

In an ideal world, I would recommend sitting down with your children to discuss their interests. However, the interests of young people are decidedly stupid so that's a non-starter. Instead, I have provided a few sensible suggestions.

Arts And Crafts
An old summer camp favourite, arts and crafts can encourage children's creativity and produce beautiful, useful items. Drawing, painting, knitting, building birdhouses -- there's

something for everyone and supplies needn't break the bank. Some of our greatest artists started off as potential hoodlums whose lives were changed the moment they were handed an egg carton, glue and fuzzy felt.

Reading
Before you laugh, consider this: your mild alcoholism is clearly an attempt to escape the drudgery of your home; children, until licensing laws are changed, cannot turn to the bottle. Good books, on the other hand, take readers on magical adventures where your kids can live the life you'd have given them if you hadn't made such poor choices.

Gardening
Whether it's cress in a yoghurt pot, roses in a flower bed or veggies in the greenhouse, growing something can teach children planning, hard work and responsibility. A particularly helpful strategy is telling them that sitting silently and watching the plants will help them sprout more quickly.

Running On The Spot
Not all kids like sports, and many child development experts feel the competition of teams can lead to thug violence. Running in place is an excellent alternative. It keeps a body healthy and in its own back garden.

Crime Solving
Thousands of cold cases go unsolved annually because police stations just do not have enough officers to sift through the evidence. Children's natural curiosity and deviousness could shed new light on mysteries and criminals that have eluded justice for years. Additionally, staring at crime scene photos for hours on end may keep them on the straight and narrow in the future.

Classical Dressage
Most kids love animals so participating in classical dressage can be both fun and educational. Supplies needed: a Lipizzaner

horse, tack (saddle, bridle, bit), clothing (shirt, stock tie, breeches, gloves, coat, dress boots, spurs and hunting cap) and a small arena.

Give each at least a week -- if it keeps your children busy, continue to encourage it; if they are still risks to society, try the next one. With a little luck, we'll find one that strengthens their minds and hearts, or, at the very least, we'll have neutralised their poisonous affect on the community until the schools reopen.

ZODIAC
There Shall Be Signs in The Sun, And In The Moon, And In The Stars

So said Jesus and you know he was very rarely wrong (save for the sandals -- even the most devout of Christians has to admit that sandals on a man is never the right choice). I myself have never been a follower of horoscopes, though I have no problem with those who are. I firmly believe that one has the right to waste time and money on whatever bunkum if it feels helpful. Clearly, millions of idiots all around the world take solace in the guidance their horoscopes offer, so there must be something to it. And by something, I mean money-making opportunities for astrologists.

I had the good fortune to spend some time with an astrologist yesterday (I suppose I should thank my lucky stars, eh?). The local WI, in an attempt to raise the intellectual capacity of its members, has started their "Einsteins of Our Time" lecture series, and I made sure to attend the first one (to let them know that I can rise above the offense that my lack of invitation to give a talk caused). The speaker was a man named Mystical Mitchel, who writes the horoscopes in our village newspaper. He was impressively academic for the first fifteen minutes, but then the ladies began to get restless, and he opened the floor for questions. As I'm sure one can imagine, among the queries were "When will I meet my third husband?" and "Are the stars to blame for my dissatisfaction with my empty life and/or my varicose veins?" His patience with their questions was admittedly admirable.

Afterward, while mingling with the old dears at the biscuit table, I was approached by Mystical Mitchel, who asked if I would join him for a drink at the pub next door. Never wanting to seem rude (even to obvious charlatans), I accepted but intended to maintain the same level of disinterest I had shown during his lecture. However, I must confess I found him absolutely charming. He regaled me with tales of predictions he had made which had come true, many of which were quite intriguing.

For example, on the very afternoon that *Thriller* first went platinum in Sweden, Mitchel predicted that "one day in years to come Michael Jackson will die and the world will mourn his passing." One cannot deny that the fact that Jackson did pass away in 2009 is just too spooky to be mere coincidence.

Being an avid follower of my work, Mystical Mitchel asked if he could offer some exclusive horoscopes to my devotees. I said, whatever. So below is Mitch's guidance, delivered directly from the stars to you, my loyal readers.

Aries: The next week will be a challenging one for you, but with a steady diet of confidence, determination and liquor, you will make it to the end of the month, having lost only your job, home or family, but definitely <u>not</u> all three.

Taurus: The stars recommend mid-August as the ideal time for your colonoscopy. Book now.

Gemini: You will have a chance to shine in a social setting. This may be the time to splurge on that toupee you've been admiring.

Cancer: The criticism you received last week about a work project will continue to sting for at least a few more years.

Leo: If the stars have told you once, they've told you a thousand times: don't take any wooden nickels. Will you ever learn?

Virgo: You may feel lonely and sad in the upcoming days. Don't worry -- it's just that you are both lonely and sad.

Libra: Don't eat any corn until the autumnal equinox. Don't even go near it.

Scorpio: You will meet a mysterious stranger. Keep condoms on you at all times.

Sagittarius: You have a 72% chance of losing a leg in the next ten days. Although it's written in the stars, it's only been penciled in, so don't start altering your trousers yet -- just make sure to watch your step.

Capricorn: The stars look favourably on your going about your regular business this week.

Aquarius: The hole you've recently dug yourself into is not insurmountable, but shutting your fucking mouth is advised as your only means of retaining any dignity.

Pisces: Your future is meh.

I hope you find his esoteric advice a comfort. And just to clear up any confusion, Mitchel assures me the whole Ophiuchus business is nothing to concern yourselves with. It only affects those who haven't already gotten their star signs tattooed on their lower backs. So if this was worrying you, breathe a sigh of relief.

Now go do something with your life.

FINAL THOUGHTS

Bienvenue. Willkommen Bienvenido. خوش آمدید. ברוך הבא. Croeso. Fàilte. Dynnargh dhis. Aloha. And welcome.

Now that you've reached the end, I've trust you've found yourself in a better place, namely, my world. It's nice here, isn't it?

I should clarify that this book -- while a thoughtful, informative guide -- does not come with a guarantee. This is partly because of the horrible shift in trust amongst the public: no one can legally say anything anymore without the threat of tort actions. More importantly, though, we must acknowledge that life is organic -- constantly changing and evolving. For example, what serves me well one day (Christopher) might not do the job tomorrow (so watch it, young man). I've tried to highlight the aspects of life you are most likely to face and to suggest ways to make the most of them. All I can promise is that it is very likely that if you follow my example, everyone -- employers, family, lovers, friends and even strangers -- will be drawn to you (in a good way), and your achievements may one day rival my own (not really, but that's the kind of thing one must say in these circumstances).

Please remember, my dear readers, that what brings me the most satisfaction in life is not the multiple awards, adoring fans and lovers nor the stacks and stacks o' money. My life is fulfilled when I help others, and I thank you for allowing me to help you today.

Yours,
Agatha